Regulating Lawyers Through Disciplinary Systems

This book offers comparative analyses on issues in lawyer regulation in England and Wales, Japan, Myanmar, New Zealand and Singapore.

It examines the lawyer disciplinary systems in different jurisdictions through diverse and comparative perspectives. In addition to enriching the literature on legal ethics, contributions also highlight areas for future research regarding the legal and other professions in different jurisdictions and the methodologies that may be applied. Chapters examine common issues faced by lawyer disciplinary systems throughout the world, such as:

- transparency of regulatory outcomes, which varies widely and provides challenges to assessing the effectiveness of lawyer regulatory systems
- whether systems tilt too much toward protecting lawyers and if a move from self-regulation to independent regulators yields better outcomes
- changes in demographics of the legal profession and regulatory changes posing challenges in longitudinal studies of regulatory systems
- disciplining of repeat actors raising questions of the deterrence goals of a regulatory system
- deviation of systems that maintain tight state control over the legal profession from both United Nations and other international norms for lawyer discipline
- the role of pro bono obligations and the discourse around legal ethics.

Regulating Lawyers Through Disciplinary Systems will be an invaluable resource for scholars, practitioners and regulators of the legal profession, while also appealing to those interested in legal and other professional ethics. This book was originally published as a special issue of the *International Journal of the Legal Profession*.

Kay-Wah Chan is Visiting Professor (part-time and remote) at National Yang Ming Chiao Tung University in Taiwan. He has written and presented on the Japanese legal profession.

Judith A. McMorrow is Professor of Law at Boston College Law School, in the United States. She works extensively on comparative professional ethics, including lawyer regulation in both the United States and China.

Avrom Sherr is Emeritus Professor at the Institute of Advanced Legal Studies in the United Kingdom. He has provided an international leadership role in exploring the sociology of the legal profession and ethics in professional work. He is the founding editor of the *International Journal of the Legal Profession*.

Regulating Lawyers Through Disciplinary Systems

Edited by
Kay-Wah Chan, Judith A. McMorrow and Avrom Sherr

Routledge
Taylor & Francis Group
LONDON AND NEW YORK

First published 2024
by Routledge
4 Park Square, Milton Park, Abingdon, Oxon OX14 4RN

and by Routledge
605 Third Avenue, New York, NY 10158

Routledge is an imprint of the Taylor & Francis Group, an informa business

British Library Cataloguing in Publication Data
A catalogue record for this book is available from the British Library

ISBN13: 978-1-032-61607-0 (hbk)
ISBN13: 978-1-032-61609-4 (pbk)
ISBN13: 978-1-032-61610-0 (ebk)

DOI: 10.4324/9781032616100

Typeset in Minion Pro
by Newgen Publishing UK

Publisher's Note
The publisher accepts responsibility for any inconsistencies that may have arisen during the conversion of this book from journal articles to book chapters, namely the inclusion of journal terminology.

Contents

Citation Information

The chapters in this book were originally published in the *International Journal of the Legal Profession*, volume 28, issue 2 (2021). When citing this material, please use the original page numbering for each article, as follows:

Introduction

Introduction
Kay-Wah Chan and Judith A. McMorrow
International Journal of the Legal Profession, volume 28, issue 2 (2021), pp. 127–128

Chapter 1

"Trusted to the ends of the earth?" An analysis of solicitors' disciplinary processes in England and Wales from 1994 to 2015
Andrew Boon and Avis Whyte
International Journal of the Legal Profession, volume 28, issue 2 (2021), pp. 129–157

Chapter 2

Disciplining legal practitioners in New Zealand
Selene E. Mize
International Journal of the Legal Profession, volume 28, issue 2 (2021), pp. 159–180

Chapter 3

The nature of the disciplinary system over Myanmar lawyers: differences from international standards and implications for international legal transplants
Jonathan Liljeblad
International Journal of the Legal Profession, volume 28, issue 2 (2021), pp. 181–198

Chapter 4

Evaluating the effectiveness of the lawyer disciplinary system in Japan: a study on "repeaters"
Kay-Wah Chan
International Journal of the Legal Profession, volume 28, issue 2 (2021), pp. 199–221

Chapter 5

Managing discourse about lawyers: pro bono and professional misconduct
Helena Whalen-Bridge
International Journal of the Legal Profession, volume 28, issue 2 (2021), pp. 223–239

For any permission-related enquiries please visit:
www.tandfonline.com/page/help/permissions

Notes on Contributors

Andrew Boon, The City Law School, City, University of London, London, UK.

Kay-Wah Chan, National Yang Ming Chiao Tung University, Hsinchu, Taiwan.

Jonathan Liljeblad, College of Law, Australian National University, Acton, Australia.

Judith A. McMorrow, Boston College Law School, USA.

Selene E. Mize, Faculty of Law, University of Otago, Dunedin, New Zealand.

Avrom Sherr, Institute of Advanced Legal Studies, UK.

Helena Whalen-Bridge, Faculty of Law, National University of Singapore Faculty of Law, Singapore.

Avis Whyte, Westminster Law School, University of Westminster, London, UK.

Introduction

This special issue brings together five papers, earlier versions of which were presented at the workshop "Regulating Lawyers through Disciplinary Systems" (Workshop) held at the International Institute for the Sociology of Law (IISL), Spain in April 2018, or a panel on the same theme at the International Legal Ethics Conference VIII held in Melbourne, Australia in December 2018. The contributors study the lawyer disciplinary systems in different jurisdictions and from different perspectives. In addition to enriching the literature on legal ethics, they also highlight areas for future research regarding the legal and other professions in different jurisdictions and the methodologies that may be applied.

Helena Whalen-Bridge analysed the "coherence" of "pro bono discourse in professional misconduct" in Singapore and found that the discourse may "complicate or enlighten" an analysis in the context of professional misconduct. Similar investigations can be conducted on the coherence of other discourses in relation to legal ethics, as well as the coherence of the professional ethics discourse in other disciplines.

Andrew Boon and Avis Whyte empirically analysed solicitors' disciplinary cases to investigate the effect of regulatory and demographic changes on the outcomes of disciplinary regulation in England and Wales. Their work may serve as a model for exploring the question of whether regulatory and/or other changes in the legal profession in other jurisdictions have an impact on their disciplinary systems or other aspects of the profession. A similar study may also be conducted in relation to other professions.

Kay-Wah Chan conducted an empirical analysis on cases of disciplinary sanctions and found the Japanese disciplinary system ineffective in deterring at least some of the *bengoshi* who had been disciplined from committing further misconduct. His empirical methodology may be adopted for similar studies on the legal profession in other jurisdictions as well as other professions. Empirical analyses, however, depend on the availability of relevant data. Because of the difficulty in obtaining relevant data for empirical analysis, Jonathan Liljeblad focused on textual analysis. "Extensive publication" of data, as Selene Mize pointed out (albeit in the context of New Zealand), facilitates researchers' assessment of the lawyer disciplinary system.

Mize found issues of concern in the New Zealand lawyer disciplinary system. They include delays and limited publicity regarding decisions. Mize argues that more extensive publication of data regarding disciplinary cases will "enhance public confidence" in the system. A lawyer disciplinary system may, however, be used in some jurisdictions in order to serve the interests of the ruling authority. In this respect, independence of the regulatory system from the state will be of paramount importance. Liljebald analysed the transplant of international standards to Myanmar's legal profession and found it to be hindered by the structure of the disciplinary system. His work extended beyond the legal ethics discourse and tested legal transplant theories. This shows that studies on lawyer disciplinary systems may also contribute to scholarship in other disciplines beyond legal ethics. It is hoped that the articles in this special issue will encourage and facilitate future research and scholarship in lawyer disciplinary systems as well as other disciplines.

Finally, the guest editors would like to thank the IISL and its staff, in particular Professor Vincenzo Ferrari and Ms Malen Gordoa Mendizabal, for their tremendous support on the organisation of the Workshop. Without their support, the Workshop would not have had the vigorous and fruitful intellectual exchange that it had. The guest editors are also grateful to Professor Avrom Sherr, the editor of the *International Journal of the Legal Profession*, for his patience and support for this special issue.

Kay-Wah Chan
http://orcid.org/0000-0001-9725-2391
Judith A. McMorrow

OPEN ACCESS

"Trusted to the ends of the earth?" An analysis of solicitors' disciplinary processes in England and Wales from 1994 to 2015

Andrew Boon and Avis Whyte

ABSTRACT
This study deals with misconduct cases involving solicitors, the largest legal profession in England and Wales. It covers a 20 year period and focuses in detail on three points during that period: 1994–1996, 2008 and 2015. These points cover different stages during the evolution of the regulatory system from what was arguably the height of legal professionalism to the post-professional system initiated by the revolutionary Legal Services Act 2007. Drawing on detailed studies of disciplinary cases we examine the relationship between professional demography and modes of regulation in determining the outcomes of regulation.

Introduction

It is now over 25 years since Sir Thomas Bingham MR identified the most fundamental purpose of disciplinary proceedings as ensuring trust in the solicitors' profession (*Bolton v The Law Society* 1994). During that time, theories of lawyer misconduct have been enriched by empirical research from many jurisdictions, including the USA, Canada, Australia and England and Wales. Different approaches, comparative accounts of disciplinary systems (Abel 2012), analysis of regulatory changes (Levin 2006) and records of individual disciplinary proceedings (Abel 2008) justify broad generalisations about, and criticisms of, self-regulating professional processes and their subjects. Despite being a jurisdiction that has moved away from professional self-regulation and experimented with new methods of regulation, there has been relatively little academic evaluation of developments in England and Wales, compared, for example, with New South Wales, Australia (Parker et al, 2010, Schneyer, 2014–15).

Research on lawyer disciplinary processes in most jurisdictions suggests that cases generally derive from consumer complaint, that professions do not seek out misconduct and that the disciplinary process reduces the number of possible disciplinary cases (see, e.g. Levin 2006, Abel 2008, Bartlett 2008 and

Lokanan 2015). It identifies the predominant subjects of discipline as middle aged men from small firms (ibid, Davies 1998, 1999, Boon, Whyte and Sherr 2013 and Boon and Whyte 2019 but see Piquero et al 2016: 582). Some of the literature explores parallels between theories on lawyer misconduct and theories on white collar crime (Abel 2008, Boon and Whyte 2012, 2019). Some writers identify lack of opportunity as the reason for low levels of offending in some groups (Abel 2008), reasoning that might apply to junior lawyers, women lawyers and lawyers working in larger firms. Few studies use a long time frame over which to examine the disciplinary system and, if they do, they do not consider the impact of demographic and regulatory change over the whole period (e.g. Davies 2005).

Our data for this study derives from published outcomes in the Solicitors Disciplinary Tribunal (SDT) over the 20 year time frame. Our analysis focuses both on the impact of the change of regulator and on more familiar aspects of disciplinary studies: who is subject to discipline; where do they work; what kinds of offence do they commit; how are they dealt with? The context is changes to the solicitors' profession over the period: from self-regulation to independent regulation, doubling of the numbers of practitioners, a trend towards larger firms and an increase in the proportion of women lawyers (Bartlett 2008, Boon and Whyte 2019). Our central question is: to what extent do these massive changes affect the outcomes of regulation relating to disciplinary procedures? Our theoretical perspective is provided by Foucault's notion that regulation in the neoliberal period prefers and encourages regulation of the self, over regimes of punishment (Lemke 2001).

Context and method

The research examines annual statistics for the whole period as set out in Appendix 1. It also looks in detail at three specific periods: 1994–96, 2008 and 2015. Material for the first period was collected by Davies (1998, 1999) using randomly selected SDT transcripts from 1994 to 1996. Boon, Whyte and Sherr (2013) conducted the 2008 study, previously published as a report, and Boon and Whyte (2019) conducted the third study. It will be seen that the three periods examined in depth are broadly consistent with the data in the appendix. Differences are identified and explained insofar as the limits of the data allow. The similarity of the methods used to examine each of the three periods enables us to look beneath the surface of the statistics.

The dramatic difference in the context between each period of study is notable. The first period fell at the end of the golden age of professionalism, during which the SDT was established by the Solicitors Act 1974. This period operates as a benchmark. The second period was marked by increasing government disaffection with solicitor self-regulation, heightened academic interest in professional ethics and the beginning of a new era of independent regulation brought about by the Legal Services Act 2007 ((LSA) commencing March 2008, see further Boon and Whyte 2019). The third represented a suitable time span after commencement of the LSA to analyse its impact on solicitors' disciplinary processes. It will be noted that the operation of the SDT was essentially the same, even though its formal status changed after 2007. Other features of the disciplinary system changed, as explained in the next section.

The 2008 and 2015 studies involved detailed examination of the published transcripts of all cases heard by the SDT in those two years.[1] Consistently reported categories, for example, the respondents' age, sex and year of admission, were recorded as quantitative data.[2] Other categories, more difficult to verify because details were not reliably reported, were also noted.[3] Because of the importance of organisational type other sources were used to establish the size and type of firm respondents came from. These sources included Chambers and Partners' Guide to the UK Legal Profession and the Law Society website of contemporary law firms. Further quantitative data was obtained from the Law Society's "Find a Solicitor/Firm" web database supplemented by web research.[4] The limitations of these data are described where relevant.

An important source of contextual data is the Law Society Annual Statistics Reports, empirical research on professional demographics published since the 1980s. These are used to contextualise the data and to identify inconsistencies. There are minor differences in the data collected for the three studies. Davies used Law Society demographic data taken from an earlier period[5] whereas we used comparative data taken from the year from which we collected our data. Further, we collected some categories of data which Davies did not, including the origins and investigation of cases, the geographic locations of respondents' firms and the fate of respondents and firms following disciplinary proceedings.

Tribunal cases in context

There was a significant change after the Legal Services Act 2007 in that the role of the Law Society, the professional body of solicitors ended. Thereafter, the investigation and prosecution of misconduct fell to a regulator established independently of the Law Society, the Solicitors Regulation Authority (SRA) and complaints were eventually directed to a Legal Ombudsman (LeO). Over the period of the study the disciplinary jurisdiction for lawyers in England and Wales was separate from complaints. It is important to place disciplinary cases in this wider context, because it is quite unlike the situation in many other countries.

Davies found that in 1995 approximately 19,000 complaints were made to the Solicitors Complaints Bureau (SCB (Davies 1998: 148)).[6] Though he did not detail the success rate of these complaints he explained that between 1986 and 1995 SCB complaints increased by almost a third (ibid). This was against a backdrop of substantial criticism of the Law Society's complaints handling (ibid: 147). In 2008 there were 14,571 complaints to the Law Society's Legal Complaints Service (2009: 10), a drop of approximately 23%. Only 1,025 were upheld (Freedom of Information Request 2010), meaning that the complaint resulted in a finding, action or sanction against a solicitor or a firm (see WhatDoTheyKnow: undated and Freedom of Information Request FOI BS 319: 2010) and compensation was ordered in only 61 cases over an eleven-month period (Legal Complaints Service 2009: 17).

Others have observed this "complaints pyramid", the attrition rate between initial complaint and disposition (e.g. The Royal Commission 1979, Galanter 1983 and Abel 1998). One possible explanation of why the high number of complaints did not result in disciplinary cases could be that the Legal Complaints Service, as a service run by the profession, operated as a funnel limiting the number of cases (Lokanan, 2015). Of around 1,000 outcomes reported to the service in 2009 only four resulted in SDT cases (Freedom of Information Request 2010). Moreover, it appears that the proportion of complaints which became misconduct cases did not increase significantly even when they were handled by an independent Legal Ombudsman.[7] In 2015 the Ombudsman received 18,126 complaints, accepted 7,033 of these for investigation, resolved 6,416 of them and made 310 potential misconduct referrals to the SRA (Legal Ombudsman 2016: 25, the report covers year ending 31 March 2016). While many complainants were therefore successful, the Ombudsman referred few complaints to the SRA as potential misconduct cases. In turn the SRA referred roughly four of these to the SDT.[8] This suggests that the independent system probably produced no more disciplinary cases than the old self-regulatory one. It further suggests that most complaints are about matters, such as service standards or negligence, which do not meet the threshold for misconduct justifying SDT action.[9]

Over the 20 year period of the study, neither the number of complaints nor the prosecution rate for misconduct kept pace with the increasing size of the profession. The number of practising solicitors nearly doubled between 1995 and 2015, from 66,123 to 133,367. Over the first and second time frame of the study, however, the annual number of respondents before the SDT remained relatively consistent, or even declined, over time. So, Davies' database for 1994–96 consisted of findings in relation to 270 respondents (Davies 1998: 143) and the 2008 study, findings in relation to 279 respondents. In contrast there were 132 respondents in 2015, a drop of 52%.

Explanations for why the significant rise in practitioners did not lead to an increased SDT caseload could lie in the growth in use of alternative methods of disposal, or in limiting mechanisms operating at the investigatory and prosecutorial stages. A number of alternative methods of dealing with misconduct have been available to regulators over the period. First, from 1985, the Law Society had a statutory power to impose restrictions on solicitors' current practising certificates (Solicitors Act 1974, s.13A).[10] Second, courts had an inherent summary jurisdiction over lawyers conducting advocacy, litigation and claims for costs.[11] Third, from around 2007 a number of potential disciplinary cases were dealt with by "Regulatory Settlement Agreements" (RSAs) by which respondents accepted responsibility for a disciplinary offence that could have been referred to the SDT and, typically, a sanction and costs (Solicitors Regulation Authority 2012a). This system became more formalised around 2008 (ibid) and potentially expanded after 2007 when the LSA conferred new powers on the SRA to issue written rebukes and impose fines of up to £2,000 on individual practitioners (SRA Disciplinary Rules 2011). A final factor explaining the declining caseload could be systemic changes occurring in the past twenty years. One of the most notable is a decline in the volume of rules. Those governing solicitors' conduct, including accounts,[12] have reduced considerably, leading to suggestions of a lighter regulatory touch (Legal Finance Professionals 2017); the fewer rules there are, the fewer opportunities there are to breach them.

Davies' data did not deal with alternative disposals. The 2008 study did not consider restrictions on practicing certificates (PCs) but did find that ten cases which might have been referred to the SDT had been dealt with by RSAs (Freedom of Information Request 2015).[13] Since some of these cases involved multiple defendants, not using such agreements would have added a further 26 respondents to the caseload. This would have taken the caseload to just over 300. As stated elsewhere (Boon and Whyte 2019: 7), the total of non-SDT sanctions imposed in 2015 was 369 compared with 26 in 2008 (ibid). This shows that the SRA did increase its use of alternative disposals after 2007 but does not exclude the possibility that the volume of cases is artificially limited by, for example, investigatory capacity or prosecution policy (see further Boon and Whyte 2019).

The increasing powers of the SRA, and declining caseload of the SDT, calls into question the continuing role of the SDT. It cost the Law Society £1,193,000 to operate in 2008 (The Solicitors Disciplinary Tribunal Annual Report 2008/9). The average cost of each case was therefore £6,312 and the average cost of disposition per respondent was £4,276. This was arguably a modest price in order to decide fairly cases that could result in exclusion from professional work. In 2015, however, the costs of the SDT rose dramatically to £2,752,000 (The Solicitors Disciplinary Tribunal Annual Report 2016: 18), a 57% increase on 2008 figures. This translated to an average cost per case of £26,210 and an average cost per respondent of £20,848. Unless there are strong policy reasons for retaining professional disciplinary adjudication, the rising cost per case ultimately calls into question their role as a proportionate response to lawyer misconduct (see Boon and Whyte, 2019).

Tribunal proceedings

(1) Hearings

Lawyers' disciplinary proceedings are a judicial process following procedures set out in the Solicitors (Disciplinary Proceedings) Rules 2007 (S(DP)R).

They require that applications be backed by a statement setting out the allegations, the facts and matters in support (rule 5(2)). The Evidence Acts of 1968 and 1995 apply to proceedings unless rules of evidence are suspended by the SDT in its discretion (rule 13(1)). Although the Tribunal can compel attendance (Solicitors' Act 1974 s.46(11)) and evidence is given on oath, written statements of witnesses can also be accepted (rule 14). In the period of research, the burden of proving charges beyond reasonable doubt lay on the complainant (*Re A Solicitor* 1992, *Campbell v Hamlet* 2005), typically the regulator.

Lawyers guilty of profitable abuses have a strong financial incentive to delay proceedings. This may explain why, despite the low acquittal rate, many of the cases heard by the SDT are fiercely contested (Rose 2014). Delay in holding disciplinary proceedings is a potentially controversial issue (Hilborne 2017), not least because, unless the regulator intervenes in a firm while charges are pending, the public may be exposed to risk for longer.

(2) Types of charges

The charges solicitors face before the disciplinary tribunal are usually very broad and based on the six core principles of the Solicitors Practice Rules (SPR) 1990 (as amended) or the ten Principles of the SRA Code of Conduct 2011.[14] As in other jurisdictions, some respondents are charged under a catch-all category, such as "conduct unbecoming", covering serious infringements not covered by the rules. The criteria for "unbefitting conduct" were laid down in *Re A Solicitor* (1972). In that case, Lord Denning MR said that mere negligence was not enough; a solicitor's "unbefitting" conduct was "such as to be regarded as deplorable by his fellows in the profession" (ibid at 815f) or "a serious and reprehensible departure from the proper standards of a solicitor as a professional" (Swift 1996:12 as cited in Boon 2014: 267 note 84). Honest and genuine decisions on questions of professional conduct would not give rise to a disciplinary offence. However, if the decision was one no reasonable solicitor would make, the only conclusion could be that the solicitor failed, unreasonably, to address the issue (*Connolly v Law Society* 2007). That is then a disciplinary matter.

For our analysis, each charge as stated on the transcript was entered into an SPSS (Statistical Package for Social Sciences) database. Therefore, if a respondent breached ten accounts rules, ten charges were entered. The number of charges was significant because at that time the SDT could impose a maximum fine of £5,000 in relation to each proven charge. In total, the 279 respondents before the SDT in 2008 faced 854 charges, an average of 3.06 charges per respondent. This compares with Davies' 270 respondents yielding 974 separate charges, an average of 3.6 charges per respondent.

There are different ways of classifying the detailed charges brought in disciplinary cases. Most attempts generate multiple categories.[15] The SDT annual report uses seven broad categories of charge,[16] incorporating 28 sub-categories. According to SDT figures for 2008–9 the most frequent allegations involved, in equal measure, Solicitors Account Rule (SAR) breaches and general "breaches", at 34% each (Solicitors Disciplinary Tribunal 2008–9: 31–32).[17] These are followed at 17% by the various "failures" (ibid).[18] For the calendar year 2015, breaches of the SAR fell to 19% of the total charges with "failures" at 29% being the largest category and almost matched by general breaches at 27% (Solicitors Disciplinary Tribunal 2014–2015: 32–33). Next came criminal convictions and irregular dealings with client money at 11% and 10% respectively, a significant increase on the 2% and 5% reported in 2008–2009 (Solicitors Disciplinary Tribunal 2008–9: 31–32).

The three studies considered here used fewer categories, with the aim of being more explanatory. This is the reason for differences between the studies and the "official" data. Davies found that account rules breaches constituted nearly 44% of the whole of his sample, failure to reply to correspondence was next, at nearly 9%, followed by misappropriation of client funds at just over 8% (Davies 1998: 144). The quantitative data from 2008 suggests that breach of the SAR was still the most frequent charge type, representing nearly 41% of the total charges brought. A further 11% of charges involved failures surrounding information and advice giving. The quantitative data from 2015 shows that 63% of cases involved financial impropriety; 60% being straightforward breaches of the account rules. The high number of charges relating to account rule breaches and compliance failures is also reflected in the international literature (e.g. Haller 2001). Based on these data, we surmise that the official data under-represents financial misconduct.

One noticeable difference between the 2008 data and Davies' related to the second largest category of charges; failures around advice giving. This category was not included in Davies' study, although "misleading clients or others" represented 4.21% of charges. Other examples might have been included in his category of delay (Davies 1998: 144). The increase in the proportion of the SDT caseload represented by advice failures might be explained by the increased emphasis on client care over the period between the two studies. The concept of client care was introduced by the Solicitors Practice Rules 1990, in a rather brief rule 15. The issue became more salient in subsequent years, partly as a result of concern over increasing numbers of complaints. Provisions requiring that clients be informed about complaints handling procedures and kept up to date on the progress of their matter, were supplemented by the Solicitors Costs Information and Client Care Code 1999. A new rule was introduced to *The Guide to the Professional Conduct of Solicitors*, the notes to which warned that serious or persistent breaches of this code "of a material nature will be a breach of the rule" (rule 13.01, guidance note 1, as cited by

Taylor 1999). We conclude that making customer service a feature of codes of conduct leads to increases in related offences.

The general consistency in major charge type over time is remarkable, but professional discipline also reflects distinctive periodic crises and remedies. Davies' research took place during an explosion of conveyancing fraud, fuelled by competition in the lenders' market. At that time, around 59% of claims against the Solicitors Indemnity Fund arose out of conveyancing matters (Skordaki and Willis 1991). Three types of offence were prevalent; using client money to support the business, theft and mortgage fraud (Davies 1999: 153–9). These problems were tackled, if not resolved, by improved mortgage procedures (Boon 2014: 403–4). In 2008 the signal crisis generating offences was the so-called miners' costs scandal, the payment of banned referral fees and abuse of conditional fee arrangements, resulting in 14 cases in 2008 alone (Boon and Whyte 2012). In 2015, there was an apparent increase in solicitors involved in client fraud (see SRA 2016: 2) and failing to secure professional indemnity insurance (PII).[19]

(3) Previous appearances

Davies did not consider previous appearances, but it was found, both in 2008 and 2015, that some solicitors appearing before the SDT had appeared before. These instances tended to have occurred either a long time previously, when the solicitor faced different types of charges, or more recently, when the instant case and the previous offences were connected. Following a finding against a respondent, the tribunal heard about these previous findings and may have taken them into account in determining the sanction. Recidivism may be further evidence of the impact of certain kinds of practice context on behaviour. It may also, as Wald suggests, be the result of failure to learn from previous discipline and internalisation of poor practices rather than "innate badness" (Wald 2009: 315).

(4) Mitigation

Before the Tribunal determines a sanction, respondents are invited to disclose any mitigating factors. In *Bolton* it was said, however, that "considerations which would ordinarily weigh in mitigation of punishment have less effect on the exercise of this jurisdiction than on the ordinary run of sentences imposed in criminal cases" (1994: 519). Despite this, mitigation was offered in most cases and did seem to have an effect; there was a strong correlation between providing no mitigation and being struck off (see next section), although this could be explained by other factors, such as the seriousness of offences or failure to defend the proceedings (e.g. *Asare* 2008). Solicitors were also more likely to be fined when accused of less serious offences which they admitted or where there was no real risk that they would practice again (e.g. *Housiaux* 2008).

(5) Sanctions

The tribunal has the power to make such order as it thinks fit (S(DP)R 2007 (SI 2007 No. 3588) rule 18), including, striking off the roll of solicitors[20] (permanently or for a fixed period), suspension from practice, fine, imposing conditions on a PC, exclusion from legal aid work (permanently or for a fixed period), reprimand and an order for payment of costs (Solicitors' Act 1974 s. 47).

A striking off order means the solicitor may no longer practise (Swift 1996: 80). The SDT is under strong pressure to strike off where it finds a solicitor guilty of dishonesty. In *Bolton* the Court of Appeal said that

> [a]ny solicitor who is shown to have discharged his professional duties with anything less than complete integrity, probity and trustworthiness must expect severe sanctions to be imposed upon him by the Solicitors Disciplinary Tribunal … In [cases involving proven dishonesty] the tribunal has almost invariably, no matter how strong the mitigation, ordered [that the solicitor] be struck off … (1994: 518b-519c *per* Sir Thomas Bingham MR)

During the period covered by the later studies, the SDT applied the two-stage test for dishonesty set out in *Twinsectra v Yardley* (2002: para. 27 *per* Lord Hutton). First, it asked whether the conduct was dishonest according to the ordinary standards of reasonable and honest people and, second, whether the respondent realised that it was dishonest by those standards.[21]

As demonstrated in the Appendix, the incidence of sanctions did differ over time. Some differences can be explained by changes in the sanctions regime. There are, however, some anomalies. One such is the relative consistency of numbers struck off despite massive growth of the profession. Striking off falls within a narrow range: the minimum being 48 in 2014 and the maximum 84 in 2010. There was a dip in the percentage for striking off in 2008 compared with 1994–6 and 2015, the difference being made up by large increases in fines and reprimands rather than by an increase in suspensions, the most obvious alternative at that time. When the LSA empowered the SRA to impose small fines and reprimands on solicitors it allowed the SDT to impose unlimited fines (SDT 2014: para. 24). Since striking off usually follows a finding of dishonesty, and even a large fine is not a substitute sanction, the use of alternative sanctions should not be a satisfactory explanation of the phenomenon.

The most common order made by the SDT in 2008 was a fine (n.102) with an order to pay costs and reprimand (n.50). At the time, fines were limited to £5,000 for each proven charge (Harris 2009, 2011). The 67% decrease in fines (n.33) and 84% decrease in reprimands (n.8) in 2015 could be explained by the SRA's new powers to impose these sanctions. It is, however, inconsistent with the long-term trend revealed in our Appendix. This shows that from 1994 the SDT's use of fines remained relatively steady at around 37% of total sanctions, then in 2007 the SDT increased its use of fines. This increase continued quite steadily, at approximately 42% of total sanctions, until a sharp decrease in 2014 which continued in 2015. This coincides with a significant decrease in the number of cases brought to the SDT. It probably also accounts for the increase in the rate of striking off, since serious cases are a more significant proportion of the smaller caseload.

When fines were imposed, they tended to be modest, despite the increase in the SDT's powers. In 2015, for example, the average fine was £15,800. The average order for costs in 2015 was £15,152, but it was not uncommon for costs to run to tens of thousands.[22] That year just over 94% of respondents were ordered to pay the costs of prosecution to the SRA. The regulator is rarely ordered to pay costs in the absence of dishonesty or bad faith since this might have "a chilling effect on the exercise of its regulatory obligations, to the public disadvantage" (*Baxendale Walker v Law Society* 2007: para. 39 *per* Judge J).

In most of the cases concluded by an RSA the costs were under £1,000. In most of these agreements the solicitor accepted a reprimand. The SDT practice of making high awards of costs creates a strong incentive for respondents to accept charges, thereby limiting the length of hearing and the amount of any costs payable. This is likely to be a serious pressure for solicitors facing financial problems or for those whose practices are in financial difficulty.

Regression analysis on 2008 and 2015 data found no significant correlation between a party's status and the severity of the SDT sanction; respondents were no more likely to be struck off if they were principals or associates. There were, however, significant correlations between striking-off and misuse of client money and dishonesty and for breaches of the accounts rules when substantial sums were involved (see also Case 2013: 96). We found some support in 2008 and 2015 for Cases' observation that the SDT sometimes avoided making dishonesty findings. This may be because the courts consider that striking off is appropriate for all but the least serious cases of dishonesty (see e.g. *SRA v. Dennison* 2012).

Respondents

The respondents' personal data available in SDT transcripts is gender, date of birth and date of admission to the Roll. The respondent's employment status is also usually noted. Where employment status is not mentioned it is generally discoverable in The Law Society's "Find a Solicitor" database. Other potentially relevant personal information, for example, the ethnic origin of respondents, is not recorded because it is sensitive personal data. Nor is such information included in the database or the SDT transcripts. Below is an analysis of the available information in relation to respondents.

(1) Age and sex

It is difficult to compare Davies' data with the 2008 figures because he used age from the respondent's First Infraction Date (FID), which he argued was a more revealing indicator (Davies 1998: 152) than age at time of appearance. The 2008 study used the more conventional age at time of hearing, but the 2015 study also looked at the FID. Noting this qualification, across our time period, most respondents were in the 40–60 age group. Interestingly the over-60s group grew, relatively, since Davies' study. In 1996 it provided only 5.79% (ibid) of respondents but, in 2008, it provided 16.7% increasing to 29% in 2015. Between the 2008 and 2015 studies however, there do not seem to have been such dramatic shifts, except possibly in the increase in the over 70s age group, which rose by approximately 6%.

The preponderance of respondents in their forties is conventionally explained by life pressures, from families and firms, finance, disillusionment and opportunity, all of which can peak in middle age (Abel 2008: 46). Solicitors in this group may also be key workers in firms and therefore under greater pressure, increasing the risk of errors and misjudgements. Because they are workers with supervisory responsibility, they have greater opportunity for serious infractions (Abel 2008: 520–21). Solicitors in their forties made up the second largest group of PC holders in 2008 and 2015. The disproportionate increase in the number of practitioners over 60 is consistent with solicitors retiring later. There may also be tendency to 'end of career' risk-taking. Further research would be needed to discover the reasons for the shift and whether it is persistent. Table 1 compares Davies' finding on the FID with that of the 2015 study.

These data still suggest that the bulk of offences occur when respondents are middle aged, but there are some surprises in looking at the date of first infraction. For example, in 2015 the FID in nearly 6% of cases occurred before respondents had reached the age of thirty and in 3.4% of cases when the respondent was over seventy.

Table 1. Age Bracket of Respondents on First Infraction Date.

	1994–6		2015		
Age	%	Nos	%	Nos	%Change
20–29	2.15	6	5.9	7	+3.75
30–39	32.6	88	16.8	20	−15.8
40–49	46.4	125	33.6	40	+12.8
50–59	12.44	34	31.9	38	+19.46
60–69	5.79	16	8.4	10	+2.61
70–79	0		3.4	4	+3.4
Total	99.38	269	100	119	

Another area of importance is gender. In the international literature on lawyer discipline, respondents before lawyer disciplinary tribunals tend to be middle aged and male (Arthurs 1970, Abel 2008). Women entered the profession in increasing numbers from 1984 (Sommerlad et al. 2010: 10) and, although many subsequently left (ibid 6) overall numbers of women practitioners continued to climb. Over the period covered, women went from around 30% of the total number of practitioners in 1995 (Jenkins & Lewis 1995: 2) to nearly 45% in 2008 (Cole 2008: 5) and then to nearly 50% in 2015 (Law Society 2016: 7, ASR 2015: 7). Yet there was little increase in the proportion of women respondents before the SDT. Davies unfortunately did not note numbers of female offenders in his sample, possibly because there were none, but in the subsequent studies the proportion of women offenders were consistent: 19.2% of total offenders in 2008 (n.45) and 20.8% in 2015 (n.25), see Table 2.

Though there was a similar "middle years" pattern in the offending of men and women, there are also differences worth noting. These differences are less extreme in the lower age groups. In the 30s age range the numbers of women and men holding PCs in 2008 are within a thousand of each other and the number of women respondents is only half that of men. In 2015 the number of 30 something women holding PCs is over 8,000 more than the number of men, but they still represent only half of respondents before the tribunal. This gap increases in the higher age range. In 2008 there were roughly one third more male PC holders in the 50–59 age range than there were women and roughly one and a half more such men to women in 2015. Men, however, represent five times the number of SDT respondents in 2008 and nearly four times the respondents in 2015. Before concluding that women make more ethical lawyers, it is necessary to consider other explanations of these data.

The under-representation of women amongst practitioners in the higher age-brackets, which contain most offenders, may help to explain the significant under-representation of women overall. If one accepts the link made by criminologists between age, opportunity and misconduct (Weisburd et al (1991), cited by Abel 2008: 41) women are less likely to be present in practice at the age when serious offending typically occurs. This may also be linked to the kind of opportunity which only those in senior positions have. The current rate of growth of female partners remains sluggish with virtually two and a half male partners for every one female (19,884 compared to 8,241 ASR 2017 as cited by Baker 2018). Nor is it possible to rule out the possibility of systemic "chivalry bias" (Hatamyar and Simmons 2004: 827) in professional disciplinary matters; a tendency of investigators, prosecutors and tribunals to agonise before prosecuting or sanctioning women. Indeed, the qualitative work in both the 2008 and 2015 studies tended to confirm Case's (2013) hints at chivalry bias (Boon and Whyte 2019: 472). However, the 2015 study of "alternative

Table 2. Sex and age group of respondents appearing before the SDT and as a percentage of the population of practising solicitors.

Age	Women Appearing before the SDT				Women with PCs as a percentage of all PC holders				Men Appearing before the SDT				Men with PCs as a percentage of all PC holders			
	2008		2015		2008		2015		2008		2015		2008		2015	
	No.	%	No.	%	No.	%	No.	%	No.	%	No.	%	No.	%	No.	%
20s	1	0.4	0	0	12,694	11.34	9,877	7.4	1	0.4	0	0	7,497	6.7	5,875	4.4
30s	11	4.7	6	5	20,321	18.16	28,308	21.2	21	9	13	10.7	19,336	17.3	19,914	14.9
40s	19	8.1	7	5.8	11,663	10.42	16,636	12.5	70	30	28	22.8	16,304	14.6	19,157	14.4
50s	12	5.1	8	6.7	4,492	4.01	8,451	6.3	60	25.6	30	24.4	13,428	12	14,263	10.7
60s	2	0.9	4	3.3	570	0.51	1,765	1.3	35	15	17	13.8	4,793	4.3	7,720	5.8
70s	0	0	0	0	57	0.05	108	0.08	2	0.9	8	6.5	742	0.7	1,290	1
80s	0	0	0	0	0	0	0	0	0	0	2	1.6				
Total	45	19.2	25	20.8	49,797	44.49	65,145	48.8	189	80.9	98	79.8	62,100	55.6	68,219	51.2

disposals" found no evidence of a propensity of the regulator to deflect women from SDT appearances (ibid: 461).

(2) Post qualification experience

Analysis of the length of time between qualification and appearance before the SDT reveals a different picture to that produced by age analysis. In our samples we found that transgression peaks in middle age (40–60), whereas the post-qualification graph indicates that the period around five years after qualification is also important (see figures 1 and 2). Although Davies calculated post-qualification time-lag to the relevant conduct, rather than to the date of the hearing, his data suggests a similar early bunching for years since qualification compared to age (Davies 1998: 152: figures I and II).

This bunching suggests a possible link between late qualification and offending. Explanations of late qualification as a causal factor could include the background of respondents, their route into practice or personal circumstances. Late qualifiers may experience difficulty obtaining a training contract, enter less stable firms or practice alone. The spike at five years following qualification may be because solicitors cannot practice alone within three years of qualifying (SRA Practice Framework Rules 2011, rule 12.4).

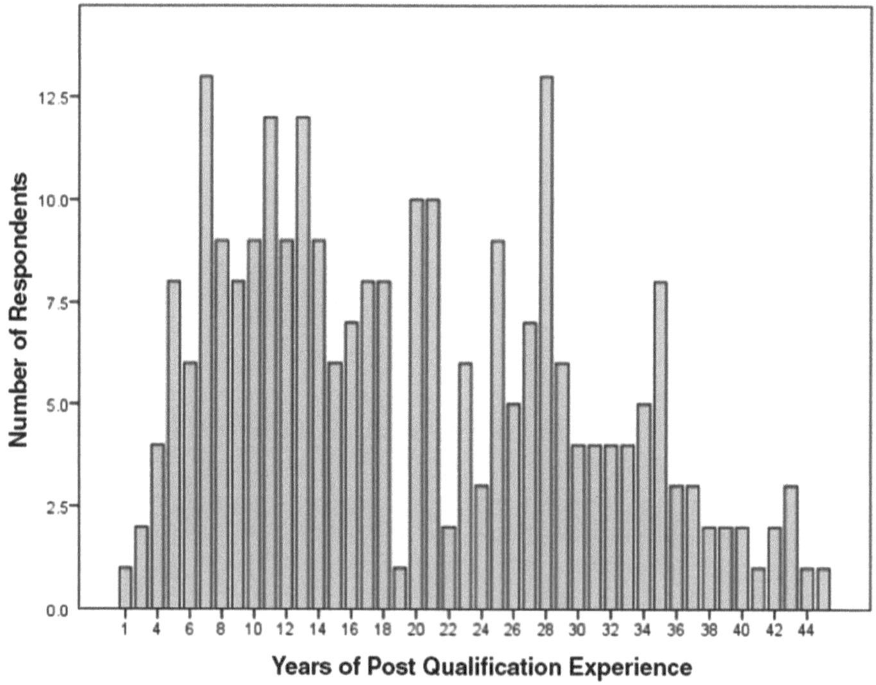

Figure 1. Number of Years of Post Qualification Experience at Appearance in 2008.

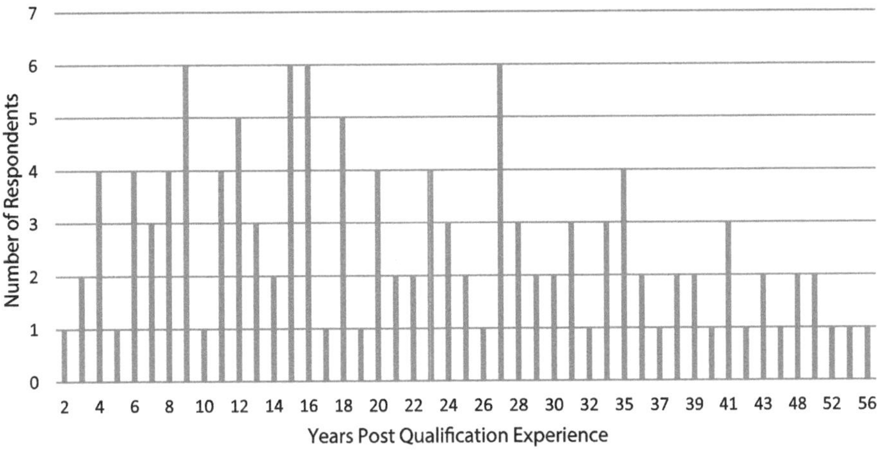

Figure 2. Number of Years of Post Qualification Experience at Appearance in 2015.

(3) Employment status and organisational type

Early criminological studies established that the type of organisation to which white-collar offenders belong is an important factor in transgressive behaviour (Sutherland 1983, Schlegel and Weisburd 1992). The same is true of lawyers. From Carlin's work on the Chicago Bar in the 1960s (Carlin 1962), numerous studies found the disproportionate representation of sole practitioners and small firm attorneys in disciplinary cases. The phenomenon is so marked that Abel has suggested forbidding sole practice as a simple way of reducing lawyer transgression (Abel 2008: 525). In interpreting the influence of organisational setting on offending it is necessary to have data on respondent status, which is reliably included in SDT transcripts, and firm size and type, which is not.

There are considerable shifts in relation to the data on respondents of different status compared to the proportion of respondents of that status in the general population. As depicted in Table 3, Davies found that sole practitioners were significantly over-represented, comprising over 50% of respondents (Davies 1998: 154: Figure IV) and only about 8% of practitioners (ibid, 155: Figure VII). Partners were, however, under-represented. In both 2008 and 2015 it was found that sole practitioners continued to be over-represented in proceedings before the SDT, but so too were partners. Another notable feature of these later data sets was that the number of non-principals, associate and assistant solicitors had climbed steadily over the period, from 8.2% of total respondents in 1994–6 to 27.3% in 2015.

These differences may be partly explained by changes in the size of solicitor practices over the period considered and, in particular, by a decline in sole practice. Davies suggested that in 1990 sole practitioners represented 7.94% of all practising solicitors (Davies 1998: 155: Figure VII). From 2000, there was a

Table 3. Comparison of SDT Respondent Employment Status Between 1994–6, 2008 and 2015.

Employment Status	Percentage by status in 1994–6		Percentage by status in 2008		Percentage by status in 2015	
	SDT Respondents	General Population	SDT Respondents	General Population	SDT Respondents	General Population
Partners	37.14	49	56.2	38.1	57	31.5
Sole practitioners	53.21	8	24.3	5.5	23.5	4.6
Associates/ Assistants	8.21	39	13.4	48.8	27.3	47.4
Others (e.g. consultants and trainees)	1.46	4	6.2	7.6	6.1	16.5
Total Population	270	53,731	279	83,329	132	91,062

small but steady annual decline in the percentage of sole practitioners from 6.8% of the total population of practitioners (Cole 2000: 19: Table 2.9) to a low point of 5.1% in 2006 (Cole 2007: 17: Table 2.9). By 2008 the proportion of sole practitioners had recovered slightly, to 5.5% of solicitors in private practice (Cole et al. 2009: 15: Table 2.9). Over the period there was also a large increase in numbers of associate solicitors, reflected in increased numbers appearing before the SDT. As Table 4 shows, however, firms tended to get bigger over the period, apparently leading to a decline in the total and relative number of 5–10 partner firms and 11–25 partner firms.

Based on Law Society statistical reports, Davies estimated that 10.7% of Principals were sole practitioners and 37.8% were partners in firms with between two and four partners (Davies 1998: 155: Figure VI).[23] In 2008, sole practitioners made up 12.5% and those in two to four partner firms were 27.5% of the total number of principals (ASR 2008: 25 Table 4.1). While the proportion of solicitors in small firms (i.e. sole practitioners and 2–4 partner firms) decreased, from 48.5% in Davies' study (1998: 155: Figure VI) to 40% in 2008, the numbers of these firms, and the proportion of the profession they represented, actually increased over the period. The increase in partners appearing before the SDT, from 37% (Davies 1998: 154: Figure IV) to 56.2% (Table 3, above) between 1994–6 and 2008 (and remaining at 57% in 2015, ibid) could be the result of marginal and under-capitalised sole practitioners and small firm lawyers, the stereotypical disciplined lawyers, seeking greater security in small partnerships. This conclusion may be borne out by the decrease in the average number of respondents per case between 2008 and 2015. In 2008 there were 59 cases with more than one respondent, with a mean of 1.75 respondents per case. In 2015 there were only 18 cases with more than one respondent, with a mean of 2.5. One explanatory hypothesis is that transgressing lawyers in small firms may involve others in misconduct.

Table 4. Private Practice Firms in 2008 by Government Office Region (GOR) compared with Respondents in SDT by GOR and as a percentage of the resident population.

Region	Private Practice Firms (per cent) in the region			SDT Respondents' Firms (per cent of total SDT pop.)		Percentage difference between GOR of SDT respondent firms and Private Practice Firms		Percentage of Resident population	
	1995	2008	2015	2008	2015	2008	2015	2008	2015
London (City & Greater)	23.4	27.8	31.9	31.2	35.1	+3.4	+3.2	*14.0	14.8
South East	22.8	14.8	12.4	10.4	10.6	−4.4	1.8	15.3	15.5
South West	9.2	6.7	7.0	5.2	8.5	−1.5	+1.5	9.5	9.4
Wales	5.9	5.0	4.5	3.5	4.3	−1.5	−0.2	5.5	5.4
West Midlands	8.4	7.9	8.0	8.7	7.5	+0.8	−0.5	10.1	10.0
East Midlands	5.3	5.6	5.7	2.9	1.1	−2.7	−4.6	8.1	8.1
Eastern	2.8	10.3	7.4	10.4	7.5	+0.1	+0.1	10.4	10.5
North West	11.0	12.0	13.4	11.6	17.0	−0.4	+3.6	12.9	12.4
Yorks & Humberside	6.6	6.9	6.9	11.6	6.4	+4.7	−0.5	9.5	9.3
North East	4.7	3.2	2.8	2.9	2.1	−0.3	−0.7	4.8	4.6
Abroad	0	0	0	1.7	0	+1.7	+1.7		
Total number of: private practice firms, SDT respondents' firms, and resident population	8,622	10,267	9,403	173	94			52,994 million	57.4 million

*The city of London represents less than 0.05%.

(4) location of practice

In order to see whether the location of firms was a factor in transgression, the firm at which the respondent worked was recoded into a Government Office Region (GOR).[24] This showed a rough correspondence between the numbers of private practice firms in GORs and the numbers of firms from those regions producing SDT respondents, as set out in Table 4. The most noticeable features of these data are that major conurbations have a proportion of SDT numbers relative to the number of firms in an area. Greater London is, for example, over-represented in both 2008 and 2015 by a similar percentage, whereas the East Midlands, the North West and Yorkshire and Humberside are over-represented in one of the periods only.[25]

A tentative explanation of these data is that areas with high populations of firms may have fewer repeat interactions between firms and hence there may be less surveillance of solicitors by solicitors than would occur in a smaller market. In Yorkshire and Humberside, for example, dysfunctional firms could be more visible. Similarly, the density of firms in the South East and no doubt, strong competition between them, may encourage reporting of suspicions about firms by other solicitors. A further consideration is that metropolitan areas may provide a cloak of anonymity to malfunctioning firms.

Consequences

The 2008 and 2015 studies tracked respondents using the Law Society's "Find a Solicitor" database.[26] This should be a reliable indicator of whether solicitors are practising; the SRA informed us that they could only be removed from the database if the circumstances are extremely serious (Burns 2012).[27] Three years after the appearance of individual respondents at the SDT in 2008, only 40% could be identified as still in practice, leaving nearly 60% who seem to have disappeared from the profession. These percentages remained high in 2015 where, a year and a half after appearance, around 70% of respondents were apparently no longer practicing and of the, roughly, 30% remaining, 5% of these did so as non-practicing solicitors. This may be explained by the fact that, in both years, these percentages include respondents who were struck off (17% in 2008 and 42% in 2015) and those sanctioned in their 60s and older (17% in 2008 and 25% in 2015) and who may then have retired from the profession. There were more respondents whose whereabouts were unaccounted for in 2008 (26%) than in 2015 (3%). In 2015 Company House checks found that some respondents had taken up directorships, generally in companies unconnected with legal services.

To ascertain how many of the firms associated with respondents were still in existence, we used the Law Society's "Find a Firm" database, supplemented by a Google search and, for 2015 firms, we also searched the SRA's "Law Firm

Search" database. We found that only 26.5% of the firms whose members appeared before the SDT in 2008 were either on the database or had their own, active web sites. Therefore, it appeared that 73.4% of firms had either changed their name, had limited web presence or ceased to exist.[28] In 2015 38.5% of the firms seemed to be still operating with 61.5% of firms unaccounted for. The SRA was surprised by this conclusion and explained it by suggesting that firms could opt out of being shown on the "Find a Firm" database (email correspondence on file with the authors). Given the disciplinary backdrop to some of these firms, it is a concern that they are given this opportunity. It appeared from a list of what the SRA calls interventions (closures) it undertook in 2008 (on file with the authors) that action was taken against 43 of the 181 firms. In 2015 the SRA intervened in 17 of the 94 firms involved in disciplinary proceedings and a further 41 of these firms closed independently.

One hypothesis for the disappearance of so many firms implicated in disciplinary proceedings is that that the financial and organisational difficulties that caused solicitors to breach professional rules in the first place, drove their firms out of business. It is disturbing that disciplined solicitors can disappear from the profession but reappear in the unregulated sector provided they are not held out as solicitors. Surprisingly there appears to have been no systematic tracking of such individuals or attempts to prevent them working for entities offering legal services.

Conclusion

From 1974 the solicitors' profession in England and Wales operated a regulatory system built around a disciplinary tribunal as part of a regime of professional self-regulation. Davies (2005) considered aspects of this system to be deeply unsatisfactory. He suggested that solicitors suspected of failings were investigated tardily and inefficiently, those struck-off for dishonesty offences were re-admitted to the roll and some went on to commit further offences. The retrospective role of the disciplinary tribunal meant that consumers often continued to be exposed, even while solicitors were under investigation.

In 2007 the LSA introduced independent regulation of the legal professions. This involved a number of structural innovations. An agency for independent investigation of complaints against all regulated lawyers (Legal Ombudsman) was introduced. Regulation of two vital areas, admissions and practice, was placed in the hands of an independent regulator, the SRA. While the disciplinary tribunal was retained as the final resort in disciplinary matters, the investigation and prosecution of cases was also placed in the hands of the SRA. It went on to introduce several changes across its areas of regulatory responsibility.

In practice regulation, the SRA required that firms nominate individuals to be responsible for the behaviour of their employees in relation to the areas of professional conduct and finance. This could be seen as part of a move towards a different system of regulation, Proactive Management-based Regulation (PMBA) (Schneyer, 2013–14), which has been advocated as a means of building the ethical infrastructure of law firms (Chambliss and Wilkins, 2002) and therefore consistent with professionalism. In the context of England and Wales, at least, we have argued that, rather, this is part of a systematic shift towards new means of "regulating the self" consistent with neo-liberal regulatory philosophy (Boon and Whyte 2019). Thus, some features of regulatory strategy are consistent with Foucault's observation that modern notions of discipline are more likely to focus on regulating the locus for misconduct, the *environment*, rather than punishing the offender (Lemke, 2001).

While PMBA has arguably showed some results (Boon and Whyte 2019), we also find possible support for our interpretation. An example is the LSA provision allowing the SRA to impose relatively small fines (£2,000 maximum) for minor misconduct, which arguably had more demonstrable impact. This new power, which was part of a suite of "administrative sanctions", was generally used with RSAs, growing numbers of which allowed individuals accused of misconduct to agree to relatively minor sanctions in order to avoid a tribunal appearance. Growing use of these administrative sanctions points to move towards a more informal and less juridical system of professional discipline. Some evidence for such a conclusion may be found in Appendix 1. Cases presented to the SDT fell below 200 for the first time over the 20 year period in 2013 and remained there for the next two years. There was also a significant reduction in the numbers of fines imposed by the SDT in 2014 and 2015. In both these examples, it is too early to say whether the decline will continue.

The new approach enabled the SRA to be more pro-active in disciplinary matters. It could deal more swiftly and effectively with minor breaches of rule, such as failure to file accounts, which are often symptomatic of deeper failings within firms. This enabled more targeted interventions across a spectrum of behaviour using a suite of regulatory controls. These went from noting and monitoring minor infractions up to prosecuting more serious cases in the disciplinary tribunal. Consequently, more cases of misconduct could be dealt with swiftly and proportionately at an earlier stage. Early action is more likely to prevent consumer harm. Our data do not suggest, however, that there has been significant change brought about by ending self-regulation. There has been a fall in the numbers of SDT cases, but it seems implausible that this has been achieved by improvements in behaviour. Indeed, some features of the profession present challenges to establishing ethical infrastructures in firms.

Over the period we examined, the largest category of SDT respondent are men in their 40s to 50s, either sole practitioner or small firm partner. This is consistent with most international data (e.g. the series of studies by Levin, 1998, 2004, 2012 and 2013 and Arnold and Hagan as cited by Sklar, Taouk et al. 2019). Law Society data (ASR 2018) shows that women practitioners now comprise 50.1% of the profession in England and Wales. Davies' data did not mention women offenders, possibly because there were none. This has certainly changed, but the number of female offenders has not increased proportionate to their number in the profession. Above we note possible reasons for this, some of which are also reflected in the international literature.

The predominance of small firm lawyers in disciplinary cases is usually explained by factors inherent in sole practice: lack of firm infrastructure, the absence of peer and hierarchical controls, business and personal financial pressures and the presence of greater opportunity for undiscovered transgression. The continuation of previous trends in relation to small firms suggests that they may also be resistant to establishing internal ethical infrastructure. These difficulties could be linked to other features of such firms such as the type of work conducted.

We found that, over time, particular areas of lawyer work are linked with disciplinary action. Although each period tended to have a category of entirely novel cases, other classes of infraction persisted. Breaches of the SAR were the most frequent charges brought to the SDT in 1995, 2008 and 2015. This complicates analysis of misconduct by area of work. Reliance on SAR charges may be because accounts breaches are the easiest offences to prove. The rules can be complex, confusing and difficult to comply with, leading to many technical breaches (Hyde 2017). The SRA's continuing efforts to simplify financial regulation (SRA 2019) may lead to fewer such cases. Each period had a number of cases in an entirely novel category. We suspect that a long view of misconduct cases in other jurisdictions would find caseloads demonstrating both predictable mundanity and unpredictable exceptions (Witte 2018, Covington 2018).

Schneyer (2014–15) argues that there is no need to end self-regulation in order to adopt a more proactive regulatory system. We agree this is so. Indeed, many of the measures used by the SRA, such as RSAs, were initiated under self-regulation. The new regime shows marked developments from the old one. There may be a question about whether a self-regulatory regime would be persistent in applying the new methods in order to achieve results reported here. Davies (2005) argued that regulators drawn from the regulated profession may be "self-deluded" regarding the transgressive propensities of their peers.

While proactive measures can be adopted by self-regulated professions, our data shows that some new systems may not co-exist easily with existing structures. There is, for example, tension between the SRA's use of administrative sanctions and the use of disciplinary tribunals. Although, over the period of our study the numbers of solicitor practitioners nearly doubled, the SDT caseload shrunk to a current low of fewer than 150 per annum. The increase in "alternative disposals", such as regulatory settlement agreements, may partially explain this. This proactivity by the practice regulator increased the cost of each tribunal case. If the SRA continues to gain increases in its power to sanction, even in the level of fine, the resulting decline in caseload may call into question the viability of a permanent disciplinary tribunal.

Notes

1. This included cases initiated in previous years and excluded initiated in but concluded after the years in question.
2. The Statistical Package for Social Scientists, IMB SPSS 19, was used to analyse the data. Each line of SPSS represented one SDT case, and variables were categorised, coded and recoded to allow the information to be collapsed and combined. All percentages cited here are valid percentages (calculated by excluding missing data).
3. For example, whether a firm's accounts books had been inspected or the exact process by which respondents came to appear before the SDT.
4. Though the Law Society's database contains details of practising certificate holders and thousands of law firms (UK and worldwide), a supplemental Google search was also made in relation to all firms.
5. For example, the national distribution of solicitors by position and by type of firm was based on the Law Society's Annual Statistical Reports 1985–90 (Davies 1998: 155).
6. Set up in 1986 the SCB was replaced by the Office for the Supervision of Solicitors (OSS) on 1st Sept 1996 (Davies 1998: 147 and note 42, p.170). This was renamed the Consumer Complaints Service (CSS) in April 2004 and in January 2007 the CSS was replaced by the Legal Complaints Service. The Office for Legal Complaints (OLC) was established under the LSA (Slapper and Kelly 2009: 327) and established the Legal Ombudsman (LeO) to resolve complaints about lawyers and claim management companies. LeO began accepting complaints on 6th October 2010, see www.legalservicesboard.org.uk/about_us/office_for_legal_complaints.
7. A creation of the LSA established in 2010.
8. Information on the source of referrals in 2015 was missing in 27 cases.
9. The potentially significant difference between justified complaints and misconduct could be material in comparing international data.
10. A former employee of the Law Society informed us that employment restrictions were widely used instead of disciplinary proceedings.
11. In 2008 the SRA successfully asked High Court judges to summarily strike off solicitors in the course of litigation (Interview 3: regulatory professional).
12. The new SRA Account Rules 2019 are six pages comprising thirteen rules (www.sra.org.uk/solicitors/standards-regulations/accounts-rules/).
13. The SRA supplied copies of nine agreements following a freedom of information request reference FOI/BS/1367 (2015) and provided details of the remaining agreement.
14. This reduced to seven on 25th November 2019 when the new *SRA Standards and Regulations* replacing the *SRA Handbook* came into force, see www.sra.org.uk/handbook/ accessed 8 May 2019.

15. Haller's study of disciplinary hearings in Queensland, Australia between 1930 and 2000 produced 81 individual charge types (Haller 2001).
16. Criminal conviction, accounts rule breaches, clients' money, failures (e.g., failure to pay counsel's/agent's fees, comply with undertaking, or provide costs information), general breaches, delays and other.
17. Note, general "Breaches" included, for example, breach of the Solicitors Practice Rules, breach of the Solicitors Publicity code and breach of the Solicitors Introduction and Referral Code.
18. Failure to: pay counsel's/agent's fees, comply with undertaking, comply with OSS direction/resolution, failure to account, provide costs information, supervise, comply with Solicitors Separate Business Code, respond to OSS/others and comply with Solicitors Indemnity Rules. By 2015 reference to the OSS had been replaced by reference to the SRA.
19. This followed the 2011 decision to close the Assigned Risks Pool, the safety net for solicitors' firms unable to obtain client liability insurance on the open market. See, SRA Indemnity Insurance Rules 2012 as amended by the SRA Indemnity Insurance Rules 2013 (www.sra.org.uk/solicitors/handbook/indemnityins/content.page) and R Collins "Why the SRA Replaced the Assigned Risks Pool" LSG 21 July 2011, https://www.lawgazette.co.uk/analysis/why-the-sra-replaced-the-assigned-risks-pool/61455.article (accessed 16 October 2017).
20. The SRA keeps a list of all solicitors of the Senior Courts of England and Wales, called "the roll" (SRA 2011).
21. See now, *Ivey v Genting Casinos* [2017] UKSC 67, which has made both limbs of the test objective.
22. This tended to happen in cases of joint liability. For example, *In the Matter of Brian William Copley et al.,* (2008) ten parties were each fined £1,000 and were jointly and severally liable for costs of £24,000. Individual respondents have also been liable for costs disproportionate to fine, such as, *In the Matter of Clive Arthur Sharples* (2008) a fine of £5,000 was handed down and costs awarded of £17,000.
23. Davies figures cover 1985–90 and are thus different to the Law Society's figures for 1995. We include the Law Society's figures in our table to ensure consistency with of use of the Society's figures throughout our article.
24. Government Office Regions (GOR) in England and Wales closed on 31 March 2011 but the Office of National Statistics retains the GOR coding. Since April 2011 GORs are referred to as Regions (Office of National Statistics: Undated).
25. Law Society Annual Statistical Reports (1995) Table 3.16 p.28, (2008) Table 3.5 p.23, (2015) Table 3.5 p.25. Location was not a factor considered by Davies and thus data is missing for 1995.
26. For 2008, tracking took place during November and December and for 2015 during June and July 2016.
27. We are grateful to the SRA, and particularly to Chris Burns, for details.
28. Firms have "a limited web presence" where they could only be found in web directories such as The Law Directory (2015) and The Independent Directory (2015). These are not necessarily up to date and are unreliable indicators that firms still exist.

Disclosure statement

No potential conflict of interest was reported by the author(s).

References

Abel, R. L. (1998) *The Making of the English Legal Profession 1800*-1988 (Washington, DC, Beard Books).

Abel, R. L. (2012) Comparative studies of lawyer deviance and discipline, *Legal Ethics (Special Edition), 15*(2), pp. 187–195.

Abel, R. L. (2008) *Lawyers in the Dock: Learning from Attorney Disciplinary Proceedings* (Oxford, Oxford University Press).

Arthurs, S. (1970) Discipline in the Legal Profession in Ontario, *Osgoode Hall Law Journal, 7* (3), pp. 235–269.

Baker, T. (2018) The future is female – women lawyers outnumber men in UK as the in-house boom continues, *Legal Business* 22 June. Available at www.legalbusiness.co.uk/blogs/the-future-is-female-women-lawyers-outnumber-men-in-uk-as-the-in-house-boom-continues, accessed 27 February 2019.

Bartlett, F. (2008) Professional discipline against female lawyers in Queensland: a gendered analysis, *Griffith Law Review, 17*(1), pp. 301–329.

Boon, A. (2014) *The Ethics and Conduct of Lawyers in England and Wales*, 3rd ed. (Oxford, Hart Publishing).

Boon, A. & Whyte, A. (2012) Icarus falls: the coal health scandal, *Legal Ethics, 15*(2), pp. 277–313.

Boon, A. & Whyte, A. (2019) Lawyers disciplinary processes: an empirical study of Solicitors' misconduct in England and Wales in 2015, *Legal Studies, 39*(3), pp. 455–478.

Boon, A., Whyte, A. & Sherr, A. (2013) *The Disciplinary Processes of the Legal Profession* (London, University of Westminster Law Press).

Burns, C. (2012) Admin Officer, SRA, email correspondence (November) on file with the authors.

Carlin, J. E. (1962) *Lawyers on Their Own: A Study of Individual Practitioners in Chicago* (New Brunswick, Rutgers University Press).

Case, P. (2013) Doctoring confidence and soliciting trust: models of professional discipline in law and medicine, *Journal of Professional Negligence, 29*(2), pp. 87–107.

Chambliss, E. & Wilkins, D. B. (2002) Promoting effective ethical infrastructure in large law firms: a call for research and reporting, *Hofstra Law Review, 30*, pp. 691.

Cole, B., Fletcher, N., Chittenden, T. & Cox, J. (2009) *Trends in the Solicitors' Profession: Annual Statistical Survey 2009* (London, Law Society).

Cole, B. (2008) *Trends in the Solicitors' Profession: Annual Statistical Report 2008* (London, Law Society).

Cole, B. (2007) *Trends in the Solicitors' Profession: Annual Statistical Report 2007* (London, Law Society).

Cole, B. (2000) *Trends in the Solicitors' Profession: Annual Statistical Report 2000* (London, Law Society).

Covington, O. (2018) Bad business: Disciplinary Commission warns of 'licence rentals', *The Indiana Lawyer* 26 December, available at www.theindianalawyer.com/articles/49016-bad-business-disciplinary-commission-warns-of-license-rentals, accessed 16 May 2019.

Davies, M. (2005) Solicitors - the last twenty years of self-regulation? *Tottels Journal of Professional Negligence, 21*(1), pp. 3–26.

Davies, M. (1998) The regulation of Solicitors and the role of the Solicitors Disciplinary tribunal, *Professional Negligence, 14*(3), pp. 143–173.

Davies, M. (1999) Solicitors, dishonesty and the Solicitors Disciplinary Tribunal, *International Journal of the Legal Profession, 6*(2), pp. 141–174.

Freedom of Information Request. (2015) Reference FOI/BS/1367 (03 March), on file with authors.

Freedom of Information Request. (2010) Reference FOI BS 319 (January). Available at: www.whatdotheyknow.com/request/complaints_statistics, accessed 5 March 2019.

Galanter, M. (1983) Reading the landscape of disputes: what we know and don't Know (and think we know) about our allegedly contentious and litigious society, *University of California Los Angeles Law Review, 31*(4), pp. 4–71.

Haller, L. (2001) Solicitors' Disciplinary hearings in Queensland 1930-2000: a statistical analysis, *Bond Law Review, 13*(1), pp. 1–45.

Harris, B. (2011) *Disciplinary and Regulatory Proceedings*, 6th ed. (Bristol, London, Jordan Publishing Ltd).

Harris, B. (2009) *Disciplinary and Regulatory Proceedings*, 5th ed. (Bristol, London, Jordan Publishing Ltd).

Hatamyar, P. W. & Simmons, K. M. (2004) Are women more ethical lawyers? An empirical study, *Florida State University Law Review, 31*(4), pp. 785–857.

Hilborne, N. (2017) Report highlights delays in SRA bringing disciplinary cases to tribunal, *Legal Futures* 12 January 2017. Available at www.legalfutures.co.uk/latest-news/report-highlights-delays-sra-bringing-disciplinary-cases-tribunal, accessed 18 March 2020.

Hyde, J. (2017) SRA relaxes rules on client account and where solicitors can practise, *Law Society Gazette* 13 June. Available at www.lawgazette.co.uk/news/sra-relaxes-rules-on-client-account-and-where-solicitors-can-practise/5061500.article, accessed 16th May 2019.

Independent Directory (2015). Available at http://directory.independent.co.uk, accessed 5 March 2019.

Jenkins, J. & Lewis, V. (1995) *Trends in the Solicitors' Profession: Annual Statistical Report 1995*(London, Law Society.

Law Directory. (2015) Available at www.thelawpages.com, accessed 5 March 2019.

Law Society. (2016) *Trends in the Solicitors' Profession: Annual Statistical Report 2015* (London, Law Society).

Lawyers Defence Group. (2011) Solicitors Disciplinary Tribunal. Available at www.lawyersdefencegroup.org.uk/solicitors-disciplinary-tribunal-2, accessed 5 March 2019.

Legal Complaints Service. (2009) *2009 Performance Update. Available at www.whatdotheyknow.com/request/complaints_statistics, accessed 5 March 2019.*

Legal Finance Professionals June. (2017) 'Draft Solicitor Account Rules 2018 Published' www.lfpro.co.uk/draft-sra-accounts-rules-2018-published, accessed 7 May 2019.

Legal Ombudsman. (2016) *The Office for Legal Complaints Annual Report and Accounts.*

Lemke, T. (2001) The "birth of bio-politics": Michel Foucault's lecture at the Collège de France on neo-liberal governmentality, *Economy & Society, 30*(2), pp. 190.

Levin, L. C. (2006) Building a better lawyer discipline system: the Queensland experience, *Legal Ethics, 9*(2), pp. 187–210.

Lokanan, M. (2015) Self-regulation in the Canadian securities industry: funnel in, funnel out, or funnel away?, *International Journal of Law, Crime and Justice, 43*(4), pp. 456.

Lord Chancellor's Department, *Royal Commission on Legal Services: Final Report* (Cmnd 7648, 1979) (London, HMSO)

Ministry of Justice. (2013) *Criminal Justice Statistics* 2013 *England and Wales.* Available at www.gov.uk/government/uploads/system/uploads/attachment_data/file/312021/criminal-justice-statistics-2013.pdf, accessed 5 March 2019.

Office of National Statistics. (undated) Available at www.ons.gov.uk/ons/guide-method/geography/beginner-s-guide/administrative/england/government-office-regions/index.html, accessed accessed 5 March 2019.

Parker, C., Gordon, T. & Mark, S. (2010) Regulating Law firm ethics management: An empirical assessment of an innovation in regulation of the Legal Profession in New South Wales, *Journal of Law and Society*, *37*(3), pp. 466.

Piquero, N. L., Meitl, M. B., Brank, E. M., Woolard, J. L., Lanza-Kaduce, L. & Piquero, A. R. (2016) Exploring lawyer misconduct: An examination of the self-regulation process, *Deviant Behaviour*, *37*(5), pp. 573–584.

Rose, N. (2014) SRA: Interventions Due to Dishonesty on the Rise, *Legal Futures* 12 February. Available at www.legalfutures.co.uk/latest-news/sra-interventions-dishonesty-rise, accessed 5 March 2019.

Schlegel, K. & Weisburd, D. (1992) Introduction, in: K. Schlegel & D. Weisburd (Eds) *White Collar Crime Reconsidered* (Boston, MA, Northeastern University Press), pp. 3–27.

Schneyer, T. (2013–2014) The case for Proactive Management - Based regulation to improve professional self-regulation for U.S. lawyers, *Hofstra Law Review*, *42*, pp. 233.

Sklar, T., Taouk, Y., Studdert, D., Spittal, M. J., Paterson, R. & Bismark, M. (2019) Characteristics of lawyers Who Are subject to complaints and misconduct findings, *Journal of Empirical Legal Studies*, *16*(2), pp. 318–342.

Skordaki, E. & Willis, C. F. (1991) *Defaults by Solicitors: Research Study No. 4* (London, Law Society).

Slapper, G. & Kelly, D. (2009) *English Law*, 3rd ed. (Oxon, Routledge-Cavendish).

Solicitor Disciplinary Tribunal. (2014) *Guidance Note on Sanctions*, 3rd ed. Available at www.solicitorstribunal.org.uk/sites/default/files-sdt/Content/documents/news/SOLICITORS%20DISCIPLINARY%20TRIBUNAL%20GUIDANCE%20NOTE%20ON%20SANCTIONS%20-%20December%202014.pdf, accessed 5 March 2019.

Solicitor Disciplinary Tribunal. (2011–12) *Solicitors Disciplinary Tribunal Annual Report 2011-2012*. Available at www.solicitorstribunal.org.uk/sites/default/files-sdt/Content/documents/Annual%20Report%202011-2012%20final.pdf, accessed 5 March 2019.

Solicitor Disciplinary Tribunal. (2008–9) *Solicitors Disciplinary Tribunal Annual Report 2008/9*. Available at www.solicitorstribunal.org.uk/sites/default/files-sdt/Content/documents/annual_report_2009.pdf, accessed 5 March 2019.

Solicitor Disciplinary Tribunal. (2000–09) *Solicitors Disciplinary Tribunal Annual Reports* 2000 *to 2009*. Available at www.solicitorstribunal.org.uk/about-us/annual-reports, accessed 5 March 2019.

Solicitors Regulation Authority. (2019) SRA Confirms November launch for new regulatory model, 20 March. Available at www.sra.org.uk/sra/news/press/standards-regulations-start-date-2019.page, accessed 20 May 2019.

Solicitors Regulation Authority. (Undated) *Issuing Solicitors Disciplinary Tribunal proceedings*. Available at www.sra.org.uk/sra/decision-making/guidance/disciplinary-issuing-solicitors-disciplinary-tribunal-proceedings.page, accessed 5 March 2019.

Solicitors Regulation Authority. (Undated) *SRA Disciplinary Procedure Rules 2011*. Available at www.sra.org.uk/solicitors/handbook/discproc/content.page, accessed 5 March 2019.

Solicitors Journal. (2008) Respect the Solicitors Disciplinary Tribunal, High Court judges are told, *Solicitors Journal*, 2 December. Available at, www.solicitorsjournal.com/news/legal-profession/courts/respect-solicitors-disciplinary-tribunal-high-court-judges-are-told, accessed 5 March 2019.

Solicitors Regulation Authority. (2012a) Decision Making Criteria. Available at www.sra.org.uk/sra/how-we-work/decision-making/criteria/regulatory-settlement-agreement-or-issue-agreement-decision-to-enter-into.page#4, accessed 5 June 2015.

Solicitors Regulation Authority. (2012b) *Code for referral to SDT*. Available at www.sra.org.uk/solicitors/enforcement/intervention-tribunal/sdt-referral-code.page, accessed 5 June 2015.

Solicitors Regulation Authority. (2011) Solicitors Keeping of the Roll Regulations 2011. Available at www.sra.org.uk/solicitors/handbook/keepingoftheroll/content.page, accessed 5 March 2019.

Solicitors Regulation Authority. (2011) Solicitors Regulation Authority Practice Framework Rules 2011. Available at www.sra.org.uk/solicitors/handbook/practising/content.page, accessed 5 March 2019.

Solicitors Regulation Authority. (2016) *Solicitors and Investment Fraud*. Available at www.sra.org.uk/risk/resources/investment-fraud.page#note6, accessed 5 March 2019.

Sommerlad, H., Webley, L., Duff, L., Muzio, D. & Tomlinson, J. (2010) *Diversity in the Legal Profession in England and Wales: A Qualitative Study of Barriers and Individual Choices* (London, University of Westminster). Available at www.legalservicesboard.org.uk/what_we_do/Research/Publications/pdf/lsb_diversity_in_the_legal_profession_final_rev.pdf, accessed 5 March 2019.

Sutherland, E. H. (1983) *White Collar Crime: The Uncut Version* (New Haven, CT, Yale University Press).

Swift, D. (1996) *Proceedings Before the Solicitors' Disciplinary Tribunal*(London, The Law Society).

Taylor, N. (Ed.) (1999) *The Guide to the Professional Conduct of Solicitors* (London, The Law Society, 8th ed.).

Wald, E. (2009) Book Review, Richard L. Abel, *lawyers in the dock: Learning from Attorney Disciplinary Proceedings*. New York: Oxford University Press 2008, *Journal of Legal Education*, *59*(2), pp. 311–340.

Weisburd, D., Wheeler, S., Waring, E. & Bode, N. (1991) *Crimes of the Middle Classes: White-Collar Offenders in the Federal Courts* (New Haven, Yale University Press).

WhatDoTheyKnow (undated). Available at www.whatdotheyknow.com, accessed 5 March 2019.

Witte, M. (2018) 2017 Survey of Indiana Lawyer Discipline decisions, *Indiana Law Review*, *51*, pp. 1181–1216.

Cases

Arnold, In the Matter of John Charles (2008) Case No. 9343-2005, http://www.solicitorstribunal.org.uk/sites/default/files-sdt/9343-2005%20-%20Arnold.pdf, accessed 26 February 2019.

Asare, In the Matter of Kojo (2008) Case No. 9766-2007, http://www.solicitorstribunal.org.uk/sites/default/files-sdt/9766-2007%20-%20Asare.pdf, accessed 26 February 2019.

Baxendale Walker v Law Society [2007] 3 All ER 330.

Blakeborough, David, Cooper, John Benjamin, Mahaffey, Jane Elizabeth, Melluish, Deborah Anne, Murphy, Neil Simon Jerome, Pendlebury, Anne Elizabeth, Pollitt, Steven John, Royle, John Michael, Schofield, Judith Mary, Sugden, William Andrew, Tracey, Malcolm Noel And Webb, Michael Francis (2008) Case No. 9853-2007, transcript on file with the authors.

Bolton v The Law Society [1994] 1 W.L.R. 512.

Campbell v Hamlet [2005] UKPC 19.

Connolly v Law Society [2007] EWHC 1175 (Admin).

Copley et al., In the Matter of Brian William (2008) Case No. 9910-2008, transcript on file with the authors.

Heer Manak Solicitors Kulwant Singh Manak, Robin Heer, Balbir Singh Dahil, Pritpal Chahal and Rajbinder Kaur Dhillon (2015) Case No. 11165-2013, transcript on file with the authors.

Housiaux, In the Matter of Paul Joseph (2008) Case No. 9792-2007, transcript on file with the authors.

Hutchison, In the Matter of DW (2008) Regulatory Settlement Agreement 14 March 2008, transcript on file with the authors.

Kettlewell, Stephen Paul (2008). Case No. 9862-2008, transcript on file with the authors.

O'Hare, Theresa Ann (2014). Case No. 11299/2014, transcript on file with the authors.

Prashar, Priya (2008). Case No. 9810-2007, transcript on file with the authors.

Sharples, In the Matter of Clive Arthur (2008) Case No. 9802-2007, transcript on file with the authors.

Sayeed Mohammed Shoaib and Wahab Shabana (2008) Case No. 9421-2006, transcript on file with the authors.

Sudusinghe, In the Matter of Priyadharshini Nirmala (2008) Case No. 9804-2007, transcript on file with the authors.

Tunstall, Claire Louise (2014). Case No. 11289-2014), transcript on file with the authors.

Re A Solicitor [1972] 2 All ER 811.

Solicitors Regulation Authority v. Anthony Lawrence Clarke Dennison [2012] EWCA Civ 421.

Storrar, In the Matter of Christopher John and four others, Regulatory Settlement Agreement dated 30 September 2008, transcript on file with the authors.

Appendix. Key Statistics on Solicitor Discipline 1994–96 and 2000–2015[a].

Table A1.

	1994–96	2000	2001	2002	2003	2004	2005	2006	2007	2008	2009	2010	2011	2012	2013	2014	2015
Struck off the roll		73	62	77	78	52	54	63	67	61	57	84	79	52	75	48	56
	44.9%	35.78%	30.54%	37.94%	35.45%	29.38%	26.47%	32.81%	31.60%	22.59%	19.93%	23.08%	25.32%	21.22%	32.47%	48%	47.06%
Suspended (indefinite & fixed period)		38	29	39	39	38	42	39	33	47	37	44	52	60	43	14	15
	16.54%	18.60%	14.29%	19.21%	17.73%	21.47%	20.59%	20.31%	15.57%	17.41%	12.94%	12.09%	16.66%	24.49%	18.61%	14%	12.61%
Fined		72	78	75	83	70	79	64	86	110	122	172	119	102	81	29	33
	37.13%	35.29%	38.42%	36.95%	37.74%	39.55%	38.73%	33.33%	40.57%	40.74%	42.66%	47.25%	38.14%	41.63%	35.06%	29%	27.73%
Reprimanded		14	29	4	14	12	17	16	20	37	55	49	36	19	18	2	8
	1.5%	6.86%	14.29%	1.97%	6.36%	6.78%	8.33%	8.33%	9.43%	13.70%	19.23%	13.46%	11.54%	7.76%	7.79%	2%	6.72%
No order/		7	5	8	6	5	12	10	6	15	15	15	26	12	14	7	7
Costs only order/ Case dismissed	0.74%	3.43%	2.46%	3.94%	2.73%	2.82%	5.88%	5.21%	2.83%	5.55%	5.24%	4.12%	8.33%	4.90%	6.06%	7%	5.88%
Total Number of Disciplinary Orders[b]	?	204	203	203	220	177	204	192	212	270	286	364	312	245	231	100	119
Total Number of 'Cases' (Applications received by the SDT / Hearings Determined)[c]	270	276	207	227	205	215	235	212	249	262	268	273 (259)	227 (227)	239 (202)	166 (125)	117 (91)	140 (126)
Number of Solicitors Holding Practising Certificates (PCs)[d]	66,123	82,769	86,603	89,045	92,752	96,757	100,938	104,543	108,407	112,433	115,475	117,862	121,933	128,778	127,676	130,382	133,376
Percentage of Applications received to Number of Solicitors with PCs	0.40%	0.33%	0.24%	0.25%	0.22%	0.22%	0.23%	0.20%	0.23%	0. 23%	0. 23%	0. 23% (0.22%)	0. 19% (0.19%)	0. 19% (0.16%)	0.13% (0.10%)	0.09% (0.07%)	0. 10% (0.09%)

[a]1994–96 figures were taken from Davies (1998: 143 and 160). The remaining figures for the disciplinary actions against solicitors are taken from the Solicitors Disciplinary Tribunal Annual Reports 2000–2015. Until 2013 the SDT collated its figures from 1st May to 30th April. From 2014 onwards, the tribunal adopted the calendar year 1st January to 31st December. For the purposes of comparison, we maintain the statistical year to 30th April.

[b]'Orders' include very small numbers where no order was made, a costs only order was made or the case was dismissed. They exclude applications for restoration to the roll, where no allegations sustained and orders with regard to clerks, the figures for wich are small.

[c]We used the annual number of applications received by the SDT as an indicator of the total number of disciplinary actions it heard. The SDT's 2010/2011 report introduced a new performance measure for the determination of hearings (the figures appearing in brackets). There are minor differences between the two measures.

[d]These figures are taken form the Law Society's Annual Statistical Reports 2001–2016. The reports collate annual figures to 31st July of the year in question. It states that 2013 and 2014 figures are not directly comparable due to changes in the way ASR data was sourced, but that the increase is consistent with growth in practising certificates holders (LS ASR 2015: 7).

Disciplining legal practitioners in New Zealand

Selene E. Mize

ABSTRACT
New Zealand's new regulatory system for lawyers has been operating since 2008. This article evaluates this system – it has several positive features, but there are also items of concern. These include delays in resolving complaints, especially at the Legal Complaints Review Officer level. Whether there is sufficient publicity on the workings of the disciplinary system, its outcomes, and the naming of disciplined lawyers, is also considered. There is a particular focus on the lack of searchable full-text Standards Committee decisions, and the requirement that the approval of the Board of the New Zealand Law Society be obtained before publishing the identity of a censured lawyer. The final focus is on people's willingness to make reports and complaints to the Law Society about lawyers suspected of wrongdoing. It has come to light recently that, at least in the sensitive areas of harassment and bullying, there is a reluctance to complain. People with knowledge of likely wrong-doing by lawyers must be willing to complain if a complaints-driven process like New Zealand's is to function effectively.

Introduction

New Zealand's new regulatory system for lawyers, contained in the *Lawyers and Conveyancers Act 2006*, came into effect in 2008. It brought a number of changes, including a new national Lawyers Complaints Service run by the New Zealand Law Society. A government-administered Legal Complaints Review Officer and a Lawyers and Conveyancers Disciplinary Tribunal were also established. While the system is working well in many ways, there are areas of concern which need improvement. There have been excessive delays, and the publicity given to disciplinary operations and decisions is limited. In addition, recent events have shown that at least some who experience lawyer misbehaviour are reluctant to initiate proceedings by making a complaint. This article begins with a very brief overview of the profession and disciplinary system, then considers these concerns.

An overview of the regulatory system for lawyers

To be admitted to the legal profession, an applicant must fulfil educational and training requirements, and have a certificate of character from the Law Society.

In New Zealand and in this article, only those who have been both admitted to the legal profession and have a current practising certificate are referred to as lawyers, and only lawyers are subject to the Law Society's Lawyers Complaints Service. The lack of regulation covering non-lawyers who provide legal services is also a pressing issue (Mize 2018, pp. 133–138), but is beyond the scope of this article. A snapshot of the legal profession on 30 June 2019 showed that there were 13,776 lawyers based in New Zealand (NZLS n.d.a, p. 12).

Grounds for disciplining lawyers

The regulatory functions of the Law Society include controlling and regulating the practice of all lawyers in New Zealand and running the Lawyers Complaints Service (*Lawyers and Conveyancers Act 2006* (*LCA*), s. 121(1)). Lawyers may be disciplined for: misconduct; unsatisfactory conduct that is not so gross, wilful or reckless as to amount to misconduct; negligence or incompetence in a professional capacity that is of such a degree, or so frequent, as to reflect on fitness to practice or to bring the profession into disrepute; or conviction of an offence punishable by imprisonment where the conviction reflects on fitness to practise, or tends to bring the profession into disrepute (*LCA* s. 241). The grounds for complaints against lawyers are thus quite broad. They include negligence and incompetence as well as intentional actions; over-charging as well as more traditional forms of unprofessional conduct; and conduct that occurs in a lawyer's private life as well as conduct during the provision of legal services.

The Lawyers Complaints Service and Standards Committees

Anyone may bring a complaint against a lawyer at no charge. Enquiries can be made through a website, and there is also a toll-free information number (NZLS n.d.b, p. 19). Most complaints are handled by a regional Standards Committee (Committee) that is staffed by volunteers, and includes both lawyers and at least one lay member (*LCA* ss. 126, 129(2)). Complaints can also follow from an investigation on a Committee's own motion (*LCA* s. 130(c)). Those dissatisfied with the actions of a Committee have a right of review by the Legal Complaints Review Officer (LCRO), who is independent of the Law Society. The most serious complaints are referred in the first instance to the Lawyers and Conveyancers Disciplinary Tribunal (Tribunal), which is also largely independent and is the only entity that can suspend or strike a lawyer off the Roll.

The Early Resolution Service (ERS) was introduced in 2013 to speed the handling of certain complaints. The criteria used in determining whether a complaint can be referred to the ERS are not laid out in the Law Society's annual report or website, but presumably include a focus on the complexity and gravity of the issues and the likelihood that the complaint might be resolved by agreement of the parties. Complaints alleging serious misconduct such as dishonesty are never referred to the ERS (Scragg 2018, pp. 54–55). Cases assigned to the ERS are referred to a specialist Committee which uses a less formal process, and may involve inviting parties to explore resolution by negotiation. By the end of the process, either a complaint has been resolved by agreement of the parties; a decision has been made to take no further action; or the case is referred to the standard track (NZLS n.d.b, p. 21). The ERS is quite successful at determining complaints. In the reporting year ending 30 June 2019, 93% of the cases referred to the ERS were resolved there, and only 7% were referred back to the standard track. Of all the complaints which were closed that year, 33% used the ERS (NZLS n.d.a, p. 17).

On the standard track, a Committee may determine the complaint following a process culminating in a hearing on the papers or, for the most serious cases, lay charges before the Tribunal (*LCA* s. 130). At any stage of the process, it may decide to take no further action on a complaint. This decision is made in a relatively high proportion of cases: 81% of all complaints that were closed in the 2019 reporting year; 81% in 2018; 75% in 2017; and 79% in 2016 (NZLS n.d.a, p. 16).

The Committee will decide whether to make an order, multiple orders, or no order. Orders are penalties or remedial actions imposed on lawyers, and must be accompanied by a finding of unsatisfactory conduct (*LCA* s. 156). If the Committee decides to take no further action, it may award costs to be paid by the Law Society to the practitioner (s. 157(1)(a)), or by the practitioner to the Law Society in situtations where no further action will be taken but the "proceedings were justified" and charging the lawyer is "just" (s. 157(2)).

In the reporting year 2019, 163 orders were made by Committees, but, other than noting the number of orders to publish name or facts, the Law Society's annual report did not provide any information on the nature of the orders, nor did the reports for 2018, 2017 or 2016. Annual reports for 2015 and 2014 show the following orders made (NZLS n.d.f, p. 8; n.d.g, p. 7):

- Payment of costs (by lawyer to the Law Society) (91 such orders in 2015; 115 in 2014)
- Payment of a fine to the Law Society (87 in 2015; 97 in 2014)
- Censure/reprimand (56 in 2015; 69 in 2014)
- Payment of "inquiry costs & expenses" to the Law Society (30 in 2015; 39 in 2014)
- Payment of compensation (26 in 2015; 16 in 2014)
- Cancellation or refund of fees (22 in 2015; 16 in 2014)
- Making an apology (18 in 2015; 15 in 2014)
- Reduction in fees (18 in 2015; 13 in 2014)
- Practical training (4 in 2015; 6 in 2014)
- "No further action but costs s 157" (3 in 2015; 1 in 2014)

- Taking advice on practice management (3 in 2015; 3 in 2014)
- Rectification of an error (2 in 2015; 4 in 2014)
- Referral to police or Serious Fraud Office (1 in 2015; 1 in 2014)
- Inspection of firm (3 in 2014)
- Intervention in practice (0 in 2015; 1 in 2014)

A principal justification for regulating lawyers is the protection of the interests of consumers (*Deliu v NZ Law Society* [2016] NZAR 1062 at [22]). It is important for the public to have specific information on orders to assess the extent to which lawyers found guilty of wrongdoing are being held to account. It is unclear why this breakdown of orders was discontinued in the more recent annual reports; it should be reinstated. The number of lawyers found to have engaged in unsatisfactory conduct should also be disclosed. Nevertheless, two things are evident from these data: first, it is of note that different types of payments to the Law Society were far more frequently ordered than compensation or other remedies that directly benefitted complainants. It is important that this information is subject to scrutiny. Using the Lawyers Complaints Service is not the only remedy available to aggrieved persons, but few of them will wish to initiate a civil suit for damages. Negotiating a settlement is another option open to them, but there is no guarantee of success. In a recent case involving sexual harassment by a partner of a junior lawyer and another employee including unwelcome verbal statements and sexual touching and bruising, unsatisfactory conduct was found and the lawyer was censured but his anonymity was protected. The fine of $12,500 and costs were ordered paid to the Law Society (*Standards Committee determination following own motion investigation of Mr X* (25 October 2018) Lawyers Standards Committee decisions (Notice of determination, ZTUVK) at [62]-[63]). This was an own motion investigation and it is not clear whether the victims sought compensation, but it might have been thought that they were entitled to some.

Second, the Committee found unsatisfactory conduct by the lawyer in every, or almost every, instance in which an order was made. There is some ambiguity, but the very large number of orders for the lawyer to pay costs, inquiry costs, and expenses to the Law Society is presumably under s. 156(1)(n), where a finding of unsatisfactory conduct has been made. The category "no further action but costs s 157" presumably refers to s. 157(2), where the lawyer is ordered to pay costs because that is just in the circumstances, even though no finding of unsatisfactory conduct was made. But even if it were referring to s. 157(1), where the lawyer receives costs, that is only 4 of the 325 orders made over these two years. If these years are representative, 99–100% of the orders accompanied a finding of unsatisfactory conduct. Thus it is reasonable to assume that all or almost all of the orders made more recently were also associated with findings of unsatisfactory conduct.

The Legal Complaints Review Officer

Following a Committee decision there is a right of review by the LCRO (*LCA* ss. 193–198). The LCRO is appointed by the Minister of Justice (following consultation with, *inter alia*, the Law Society). They must have significant relevant experience but must not be a lawyer while serving as LCRO (*LCA* s. 190(1)). In reviewing Committee actions, the LCRO and their assisting Deputies and delegates have broad powers to conduct investigations and to make inquiries (*Stewart v LCRO* [2015] NZHC 916 at [68]-[69]). The hearing process is informal, inquisitorial and robust, and involves the LCRO coming to their own view on a complaint and on the Committee's decision, rather than needing to be deferential to the view of the Committee (*Deliu v Connell* [2016] NZAR 475; [2016] NZHC 361 at [2]). The LCRO can make any order that a Committee can make, and also can order the Committee to reconsider, or refer a matter to the Tribunal. There is no right of appeal from a decision of the LCRO; judicial review is the only further recourse (*Ellis v LCRO* [2014] NZAR 220; [2013] NZHC 3514 at [46]).

In the most recent reporting year, 62.1% of the Committee decisions were confirmed on review by the LCRO; 11.2% were settled, withdrawn, or there was no jurisdiction; 11.8% were reversed or reversed in part; 11.1% were modified (for example, by changing a finding or penalty); and 3.8% were referred back for reconsideration by the Committee (LCRO n.d.a, pp. 7–8). (These percentages are drawn from the numerical data; the graph in the report contains an error and under-reports the incidence of modified decisions.) With a total of 22.9% of the reviews resulting in a change or reconsideration, the impact of the LCRO is clear. The results for previous years were similar, with 21.4% in 2018, 17.5% in 2017, 19.9% in 2016, and 24.0% in 2015 (LCRO n.d.d, pp. 7–8; n.d.k, pp. 6–7; n.d.e, pp. 7–8). This rate might seem high. Committees are composed of at least two lawyers, who are volunteering their time on top of the demands of their legal practices, and at least one lay member. By contrast, the LCRO is a full-time specialist in professional standards and discipline. Allowing anyone disagreeing with a Committee decision to have a review by the LCRO ensures that there will be a large number of reviews but provides an added layer of security to the disciplinary process.

The LCRO has recently suggested a number of possible reforms to be considered when the regulatory process is next reviewed (n.d.a, pp. 3–4). These include possible procedural changes, and whether unsatisfactory conduct remains the best standard as it covers both minor and serious breaches.

The Disciplinary Tribunal

The Tribunal is administered by the Department of Justice. The Chair and Deputy Chair are appointed by the Governor-General on the recommendation of the Minister (*LCA* s. 230(2)). Each must have had at least seven years' experience practicing as a lawyer, but must not be a current practioner (*LCA* s. 230(1)). In addition, the Tribunal has between 7 and 15 lawyer members, and between 7 and 15 lay members, who are also appointed by the Governor-General (*LCA* ss. 228, 233(1)). The Law Society provides funding and selects the lawyer members (*LCA* s. 233(2)). Only the Tribunal may make a finding of misconduct, or suspend or strike off a practitioner (*LCA* s. 244(2)). Decisions and orders may be appealed to the High Court (*LCA* s. 253). Other than awards of costs (the most common orders) and one unspecified "other", all orders made by the Tribunal in the last seven reporting years are shown in Table 1. Multiple orders in a case are common.

Table 1 does not show lawyers who were struck off by the courts (there were two in 2016) (NZLS n.d.a, p. 19). The Tribunal's annual report for 2019 has not been published yet, but the Law Society's 2019 report for regulatory activities shows that there were 40 complaints referred to the Tribunal, with 5 lawyers struck off and 5 suspended. This is consistent with past years.

Having provided a basic overview of the system, the next section addresses concerns about its operation in more depth.

Concerns

Delays in resolutions of complaints and reviews

Standards Committees

There has been a clear increase in the amount of time taken to close complaints at the Committee level in the past reporting year. The total number of closed complaints was 1272. Of this total, 32.6% were closed using the early resolution ERS track. This percentage is slightly less than 2018 with 36.8% and 2017 with 40.8% (NZLS n.d.a, pp. 16–17). On average, it took 67 calendar days for complaints to be closed using the ERS in 2019 (NZLS n.d.a, p. 17). This is up sharply from the 2018 figure of 34 days and the 2014–2017 average of 30.5 days (NZLS n.d.b, p. 27). No explanation for this increased time is given in

Table 1. Final orders made by the Disciplinary Tribunal by reporting year.

	2018	2017	2016	2015	2014	2013	2012
Cases disposed of by Tribunal	35	25	28	56	35	32	26
Struck off Roll	5	4	1	12	8	7	8
Suspended	10	10	6	14	10	6	4
Censure	11	9	18	19	8	11	9
Pay fine to Law Society	5	6	10	3	3	4	4
Pay compensation/refund monies paid	4	1	5	8	11	9	2
Not able to practice on own account	2	1		3	2		1
Restriction on employment	1	1	1	2	2	3	1
Undergo training/education	2	1		4			1
Supervision/mentoring/advice to be taken	1		3	5	2	1	2
Apologise to complainant				3	2	2	

Sources: Clarkson (n.d.a, p. 8; n.d.b, p. 7; n.d.c, p. 7; n.d.d, p. 6; n.d.e, p. 5; n.d.f, p. 5; n.d.g, p. 4).

the annual report. The trend towards fewer cases using ERS, and the recent doubling in time taken on that track, is concerning. More time was also taken, on average, to close complaints on the standard track. The 2019 average was 254 days, compared to 222 days in 2018, 231 in 2017, and 242 in 2016 (NZLS n.d.a, p. 17; n.d.c, p. 17; n.d.d, pp. 19–20). If delays continue to mount, changes may need to be made.

The Legal Complaints Review Officer

A major problem for New Zealand's discipline system has been a bottleneck involving extremely lengthy delays in resolving applications for review of Committee decisions by the LCRO. The backlog of reviews has been subject to severe criticism. Over the last 10 years, applications for review have been made for between 16.4% and 21.1% (mean 18.6%) of Committee decisions (LCRO n.d.a, p. 6; n.d.b, p. 5; n.d.d, p. 6; n.d.k, p. 5; n.d.e, p. 6; n.d.j, p. 5; n.d.h, p. 7; n.d.i, p. 8; n.d.g, p. 9; n.d.f, p. 7). No statistics have been made available on the average length of time required for these reviews to be completed, but the number of new applications for review exceeded the number of completed reviews in almost every year before 2017, resulting in a very large backlog of uncompleted reviews. In the year ending in June 2016, 271 reviews were completed, but 600 were left outstanding. No data were presented that year showing how long the incomplete reviews had been pending, but in the following year, of the 532 reviews which remained open at the end of the reporting year, it was reported that 28.2% had been launched more than two years earlier, and 12.8% of the incomplete reviews had been launched more than three full years earlier (LCRO n.d.c, p. 9).

As these reviews remained open at the time of the report, it is unclear how much additional time would elapse before the reviews were finally completed. Further, to get a complete picture of the time taken for resolution of a complaint against a lawyer where there is an application for a review, it must be remembered that the delay at the LCRO stage, which at times exceeded three full years, is additional to the time taken by the Committee. The available data show that the average time for all (ERS and non-ERS) Committee resolutions was 159 days in 2019, but was sometimes much higher: it exceeded 12 months in approximately 10% of the cases (NZLS n.d.a, p. 17). The fact that applicants are given only 30 working days to apply for review or lose their opportunity forever (*LCA* s 198(b)) stands in stark contrast to the ensuing years of time some have had to wait for a final determination.

There has been significant improvement in delays at the LCRO stage since 2017. The LCRO has no discretion to refuse and must conduct a review following every application (*LCA* s 199), but the LCRO was recently given the power to conduct hearings on the papers and to strike out applications for review without a hearing in certain circumstances (*Tribunals Powers and Procedures Legislation Act 2018* ss 121(2), 120). These new powers, along with new staffing rules and other improvements, have helped the LCRO to progress applications more expeditiously (LCRO n.d.a, p. 2).

In 2017 the LCRO began to reliably complete more reviews than new applications came in, slowly dropping the backlog. For the year ending in June 2019, the number of incomplete reviews had dropped to 244 (from with a high of 626 in 2014) (LCRO n.d.a, p. 9; n.d.j, p. 8). Nevertheless, the most recent available figures show that 64% of LCRO reviews still took more than 12 months to complete (LCRO n.d.a, p. 7). Of the 244 reviews that remained open in June 2019 (LCRO n.d.a., p. 9):

- 59.8% ($n = 146$) had been lodged in the previous 12 months
- 28.7% ($n = 70$) had been lodged between July 2017 and June 2018
- 11.4% ($n = 24$) had been lodged prior to July 2017

Thus even with the significantly improved turnover, more than 10% of all reviews are still incomplete after a wait of more than two full years.

The Disciplinary Tribunal

The Tribunal's delay statistics show only the number of cases in hand at the beginning of the reporting year, the number of new cases, and the number of cases disposed. These data show a rough equivalence between new cases and completed cases to June 2018. No data have been released for the last 24 months, possibly due to Covid-19 lockdowns. At one point, the Chair noted that complaints against two lawyers had been in hand for more five years, delayed by the need to await resolution of criminal charges against them (NZLS n.d.f, p. 2). The Tribunal could give a clearer picture of delays by tracking the time from receiving a referral to final determination and releasing that data as averages or in bands.

The importance of expeditious resolution of complaints

Delay is a very significant detrimental factor. For the public, practical consequences may include a perception that lawyer misbehaviour is not being constrained, with a corresponding undermining of public faith in the system and in lawyers. There has been a steady drop in applications for LCRO review, from a peak of 384 in 2013 to only 208 in 2019 (LCRO n.d.a, p. 5; n.d.h, p.6). There could be many reasons for this drop, but if publicity about the sizeable delays at the LCRO level has been a factor, this burdens the statutory rights of those entitled to a review, and also could lead to further stress on the LCRO's office if the recent successful attempts to speed up the process encourage increased numbers of applications.

For lawyers, a delay may mean going unpaid for years, as actions to recover fees that are subject to complaint or review are barred (*LCA* s. 161(1)). Disciplinary delays can compromise fairness, as the Court of Appeal recognised:

"Delay can obviously prejudice fair hearing rights and cause staleness. Delay can amount to an abuse of process" (*Orlov v Auckland Lawyers Standards Committee and Or* [2013] NZCA 230 at [107]). Practitioners are kept in the stressful situation of being under threat of sanction until complaints are fully resolved. The then Executive Director of the Law Society pointed out that "worry and stress caused by waiting for years for an LCRO decision is unfair on everyone. What could be a world-leading professional system is let down by these problems" (NZLS n.d.c, p. 3). In some cases, defendant lawyers might be responsible for significant delay, for example by making unmeritorious procedural applications or seeking interlocutory judicial review (Clarkson n.d.a, pp. 2–3). There is no indication that this is a common problem, however, and there are mechanisms to discourage it, such as interim suspension, which is available for charges made or referred to the Disciplinary Tribunal (*LCA* s 245).

While lengthy delays are undesirable, there are places in the world with equal or worse waits. A 2017 nationwide survey of the United States shows wide variations between states, with the extremes rivalling or exceeding New Zealand. In Virginia, for example, the average time from receipt of a complaint to the filing of formal charges was 361 days, and then the average time from filing charges to imposition of a public sanction was an additional 405 days (ABA 2019 chart VI). (There were much smaller delays for complaints that were summarily dismissed or closed after an investigation, but the delay associated with imposition of private sanctions was only a few days less than for public sanctions.) Maryland was even slower, with an average estimated time of 365 days from receipt of the complaint to filing charges, and another 547 days from filing charges to imposition of a public sanction. These figures are not totally unlike the situation where there is a lengthy delay at both the Committee and LCRO levels. In fact, the delays in those two states are greater because they are average times, not outliers. There were also American states with fairly short times, including Mississippi with an average delay of 180 days to the filing of formal charges, and then another 90 days to the imposition of public or private sanctions.

England set, and met, a target of issuing proceedings within 7 calendar days of receipt of the Originating Application in 85% of cases (Solicitors Disciplinary Tribunal 2018, p. 38). The targets for the period from issue of proceedings to determination of the application was for 60% to take less than 6 months, 20% of cases 6–9 months, 15% of cases 9–12 months, and the remaining 5% to take from 12 to 24 months (p. 39). Making meaningful international comparisons is difficult as disciplinary systems around the world vary greatly (for example, not all jurisdictions permit reviews or allow them as of right as does New Zealand), and record-keeping also varies. Nevertheless, these comparators show that New Zealand is not alone in experiencing sizeable delays.

A lack of transparency and publicity

This section addresses several aspects of transparency and publicity associated with proceedings against lawyers, including: publicity for determinations; identification of lawyers against whom complaints have been made; publication of aggregate data in annual reports; and public perceptions of undue secrecy.

Publicity for determinations

Tribunal proceedings are held in public unless the Tribunal is of the opinion that it would be proper to hold all or part of the hearing in private (*LCA* s. 238). Reports of determinations are published on the Internet unless there is good reason not to do so (*LCA* s. 239B). There is a presumption in favour of publication, and most judgments are readily available.

The Committees and LCRO are much less open. Committee hearings are conducted on the papers unless the Committee directs otherwise, with not even the parties or their representatives permitted to appear (*LCA* ss. 153(1), (6)). LCRO reviews are conducted in private (*LCA* s. 206(1)), and may be conducted on the papers, without the parties' consent, if the Review Officer views that as adequate (*LCA* s. 206(2)). Data on the number of Committee hearings or reviews held on the papers is not available. Publication of LCRO and Committee determinations only occurs if, consistent with natural justice, it is considered to be necessary or desirable in the public interest (*LCA* ss. 142(1)-(2), 206(3), 206(4)).

The LCRO routinely publishes decisions on the Internet "for interest and educational purposes with all names and identifying details removed" (LCRO n.d.g, p. 11). As of 1 June 2020, 1020 searchable full text decisions were available on the Ministry of Justice website (NZ Ministry of Justice n.d.). A random sampling revealed that the vast majority were anonymised by using fictitious names. In late 2018, the LCRO was given the power to suppress evidence and witness names, subject to appropriate conditions (*LCA* s. 206A). This power is likely to encourage publication by enabling release of certain details while retaining protection for others.

Although applying the identical statutory standard of public interest, in practice the Committees have taken a radically different approach from the LCRO's. Committees almost never release a full text decision, and publish short decision summaries for only a small number of cases. Unlike the Tribunal and LCRO, there is no search function for Committee case summaries on the website, making it very difficult to find cases that are relevant to a particular rule, legal concept, or fact pattern. Again unlike the Tribunal and LCRO, which keep their decisions online indefinitely, Committee summaries remain available online on the official website for only three years (NZLS 2017), although they are also published in *LawTalk* so could be accessed by looking at back issues of that periodical.

From 2015 to 2019, the publication of anonymous short case summaries was ordered by a Committee, on average, only 37 times per year, when they resolved an average of 1436 cases per year. Thus there was publicity for only a tiny fraction of the total number of cases, with a publication rate of approximately 2.6%. This has recently dropped even further as no case summaries were released online between 2 August 2019 and late March 2020 when the Covid-19 lockdown began. The LCRO's publication rate towered over the Committees' publication rate even before this gap: the LCRO published an average of 93.4 mostly anonymised full decisions from 2015 to 2019, out of an average of 281.1 decisions per year in total, yielding a publication rate of 33.2%.

It might be thought that the discrepancy between publication rates can be explained by the Committees needing to deal with some obviously non-meritorious complaints that can be dealt with quickly, where publication would be of no benefit. While this may be a partial explanation, the LCRO also reviews some obviously non-meritorious complaints. It is also clear that Committees are reluctant to order publication even for meritorious cases. As noted earlier, while the relevant data have not been released for several years, it is clear that all or almost all of the orders were accompanied by findings of unsatisfactory conduct. Yet there was an order for publication of an anonymised summary of the facts and holding in only 32 cases, as shown in Table 2.

No publication of even an anonymised case summary occurred in as many as 89% of the cases where both unsatisfactory conduct was found and the Committee exercised its discretion to make some form of order. Even if some of these cases did not involve a finding of unsatisfactory conduct, or there were multiple orders in single cases, the publication rate is very low.

By nature, summaries omit details. Publication of the full decisions has no disadvantages other than mild administrative expense, and serves many useful functions. First, it provides information to the profession on behaviour that will constitute grounds for discipline. Terms such as "misconduct" and "conduct unbecoming" lack specificity in the form of concrete prohibitions, and can be subject to varying interpretations. Case reports can help resolve this ambiguity and provide guidance for others. A Law Society General Manager acknowledged their educational value, and even speculated that an observed drop in the number of complaints against lawyers might be due, in part, to improved lawyer behaviour following such education (NZLS n.d.e,

Table 2. Orders and publication decisions made by Standards Committees.

Year ending	Complaints closed	Orders made	Publication of case summary	Publication of name
30 June 2019	1272	163	32	1
30 June 2018	1319	183	35	7
30 June 2017	1467	183	50	5
30 June 2016	1595	170	41	4
30 June 2015	1529	186	27	4

Sources: New Zealand Law Society (n.d.a, p. 16).

p. 3). For this advantage to be fully realised, the online decisions need to be fully searchable. A second advantage is that case reports educate the public. Those members of the public who are motivated to seek out decisions posted online will receive accurate information about appropriate conduct for lawyers, which is particularly beneficial for those who may be considering making their own complaints about legal services they have received.

Third, publicity promotes accountability in many ways. Publication of full decisions instead of short summaries can prompt decision writers to craft clear and persuasive judgments, which are particularly important as parties and the public are not allowed to attend hearings. As the High Court has recognised: "Members of the public who entrust their personal affairs to legal practitioners are entitled to know that a professional disciplinary body will not treat lightly serious breaches of expected standards … ." (*Daniels v Complaints Committee 2 of the Wellington District Law Society* [2011] 3 NZLR 850 at [24]). Extensive publication provides researchers with the data needed to meaningfully assess how well disciplinary systems are working in New Zealand. If too much lenience is shown towards lawyers, publicity enables this to be identified and corrected. Not only does widespread publication of decisions show that complaints are being adjudicated fairly, it also protects the reputation of the profession.

Committees should take an approach similar to that of the LCRO, and release most decisions in searchable full text format with identifying details stripped if appropriate.

Identifying lawyers

Practitioners are identified in published Tribunal decisions unless a suppression order has been made (*LCA* s. 240). Identity suppression for offenders has a long history in New Zealand (Gay 2019). While it has been scaled back in the last few decades, suppression is still granted occasionally. The High Court in *Daniels* held that private interests, including the health and rehabilitation of the practitioner and effects on the practitioner's family and their wellbeing, should be weighed against public interests, including protection of the public, its right to know, and maintaining the reputation of the profession for other lawyers and public confidence in the disciplinary system (*Daniels v Complaints Committee 2 of the Wellington District Law Society* [2011] 3 NZLR 850 at [54]-[59]). From 2014 to 2017, permanent name suppression was granted in a majority of the applications: 16 out of 29 (Clarkson n.d.b, p. 7; n.d.c, p. 7; n.d.d, p. 7; n.d.e, p. 4). Suppression was ordered four times the following year, but the number of applications was not disclosed (Clarkson n.d.a, p. 8).

The LCRO may direct publication of such decisions as are necessary or desirable in the public interest (*LCA* s. 206(4)). This provision presumably covers naming the lawyer who was the subject of the complaint, even though that is not mentioned. As noted above, the LCRO has adopted the approach of publishing decisions in a way that does not identify individuals. Decisions posted on the LCRO website usually have all names and identifying details removed (LCRO n.d.g, p. 11).

Before a Committee may publish the name of a lawyer who is the subject of a complaint, it must determine that doing so is necessary or desirable in the public interest (*LCA* s. 142(2)), make a censure order, and obtain the prior approval of the Board of the Law Society (*Lawyers and Conveyancers Act (Lawyers: Complaints Service and Standards Committees) Regulations 2008 (Regulations)*, reg 30(1)). The impact of publication on the interests and privacy of the complainant, other affected persons and the censured person must be taken into account (*Regulations*, reg 30(2)). The failure to expressly censure a lawyer first has prevented publication of their identity even in cases where the Law Society, Committee and LCRO all agreed that publication would be in the public interest (*New Zealand Law Society v B* [2013] NZAR 970). Names of lawyers involved in determinations are rarely publicised. As shown previously in Table 2, there was an order for publication of the lawyer's name in only a handful of cases in each recent year, amounting to less than 1% of all closed cases and less than 5% of the times that a Committee made an order. Annual reports no longer contain information on the number of lawyers censured. Data presented earlier showed that there were 56 orders of censure or reprimand in 2015 and 69 in 2014, representing between 3.7% and 3.9% of complaints closed. If the rate were the same for the most recent years, there would have been 48, 50, 56 and 61 lawyers censured or reprimanded in the last four years, yet only 1, 7, 5 and 4 names were published. There must be a significant number of practitioners who have been found to be seriously at fault but who remain in practice and interacting with members of the public.

Secrecy puts the public at risk. Unsatisfactory conduct encompasses a lack of acceptable competence, which obviously can hurt clients' interests (*LCA* s. 12 (a)). Anonymised Committee case summaries show serious issues, including a failure to comply with trust account regulations that caused direct loss to a client; overcharging; failing to respond to client enquiries; acting in a position of conflicting interests; and wilful obstruction of a disciplinary investigation (Lawyers Complaints Service 2018). The identity of the practitioners involved should not have been concealed absent compelling justification.

Publicising the identity of wrongdoers serves many other interests as well. It can encourage others wronged by the same practitioner to come forward. It removes suspicion from other lawyers. Knowledge that misbehaviour could easily lead to public exposure may serve to deter wrongdoing. It can serve a retributive purpose as well (although this is not the main focus of the disciplinary system, which is instead protection of the public and the profession). As noted earlier, there are countervailing interests that must be considered. Nevertheless, the interests of a lawyer who knowingly misbehaved are arguably not entitled to the same degree of deference as the interests of clients or innocent members of the profession who were negatively affected by the lawyer's behaviour, or who might be so affected in the future.

Decisions on identity suppression should include consideration of individual circumstances and continue to be made on a case-by-case basis. The goal of decision-makers should be to have as much publicity as possible, consistent with due consideration for the interests of offending lawyers. The infrequency of publishing the identity of lawyers censured by Committees may be due in part to the cumbersome requirement of first obtaining the approval of the Law Society Board. This regulation needs to change. It may be interpreted by the public as favourtism towards lawyers. To protect the public and maintain its confidence, Committees should be able to decide whether to publicise a lawyer's identity, subject to a stay if a review by the LCRO is sought.

Aggregate data

The statistical data published in annual reports by the Law Society, LCRO and Disciplinary Tribunal fulfil the regulatory requirements (see *LCA* ss. 76, 224, 259). They provide considerable information on the handling and resolution of complaints, however, as has been noted, they do not contain all of the information which would be useful to know. Mention of certain types of absent data has been made above, for example, the number of practitioners found each year by the Committees to have engaged in unsatisfactory conduct. This information should be linked to penalties and orders imposed.

Some of the missing information used to be provided, but has been dropped from more recent reports, usually for several years. As was mentioned above, no breakdown of the type of orders made by the Committees has been made since 2015. There used to be information on the number of parties voluntarily agreeing that their LCRO reviews could be done on the papers (LCRO n.d.i, p. 10). This provides evidence of the perceived importance for parties of holding face-to-face hearings, which could be useful now that both the LCRO and the Tribunal have recently been given the power to hold hearings on the papers without the parties' consent (*LCA* ss. 206(2), 238A). Other valuable information was never in the reports. For example, information has been provided on the types of claims that are made at the Committee level (eg negligence, overcharging), but not on the success rates for each category, or the results of those claims (eg compensation, no further action).

Compiling and presenting fuller information on the workings of the disciplinary system would increase costs, but it would be justified as it would enhance accountability; inform further decision-making; eliminate any possible perception that important information is being hidden; and enhance public confidence in the regulatory process.

Public perceptions of inappropriate secrecy

Certain events have ignited public dissatisfaction with perceived secrecy by the Law Society. In 2018, very significant media attention was brought to bear on claimed sexual wrong-doing by lawyers. One situation involved detailed alleged sexual harassment and assault of four or five young female summer law clerks at one of the country's most prestigious law firms. The events had taken place two years earlier, but the public did not become aware of them until journalists broke the story (Borissenko & Reid 2018). The law firm involved had conducted an internal investigation, and the partner and solicitor who were accused ultimately left the firm, but the firm continued working with the former partner until after the public became aware of the situation (Bazley 2018). The firm subsequently commissioned an external independent review (Borissenko 2018).

After the story broke in the media, the Law Society confirmed that no one reported the matter to it until one of the law clerks came forward at least eight months after the events in question (Hancock, Reid & Borissenko 2018). The Society would not confirm how many reports of lawyer wrongdoing and formal or informal complaints were ultimately made. The Law Society President at the time, Kathryn Beck, did acknowledge that the one law clerk who was known to have come forward did so in confidence, and did not want the matter taken any further. While one of the functions of Committees is "to investigate *of its own motion* any ... allegation ... or other matter that appears to indicate that there may have been misconduct or unsatisfactory conduct on the part of a practitioner" (*LCA* s. 160(c), emphasis supplied), it was reported that Beck said that the Society could not conduct its own investigation on the allegations, as "we will always respect the views and the rights of a victim who says they don't want to participate in that process" (Borissenko 2018). Nevertheless, Beck acknowledged that there was a "culture of silence" and that the Law Society at that time had not done enough to address sexual harassment and bullying in the profession (Borissenko 2018).

Andrew Logan, a Vice-President of the Law Society, called 2018 a "watershed year in the history of the legal profession in New Zealand" (Logan 2018). He acknowledged that the "profession has had its reputation badly damaged in the eyes of the public and our stakeholders". As one news source pointed out, the "secrecy surrounding what actions have been taken since the Law Society became aware of the allegations raises the question around the level of confidence people considering complaining about sexual assault can have in the system which deals with it" (Hancock, Reid & Borissenko 2018). The Law Society was in a difficult position, however, as the information sought was confidential by statute and/or past practice. It subsequently surveyed the profession and appointed a Working Group "to enable better reporting, prevention, detection, and support in respect of sexual harassment, bullying, discrimination and other inappropriate workplace behaviour within the legal profession" (NZLS

Working Group 2018). It has announced plans to make a number of changes to processes for reporting and taking action on sexual harassment and bullying (NZLS 2018). The Law Society has also announced that it is commissioning an independent, wide-ranging review of its structure and function (NZLS 2019). The decision to conduct an independent review reflects, amongst other things, the constraints that the current legislation places on the Law Society's ability to be transparent about its complaints process and to deal with a broad range of unacceptable behaviour, including complaints of sexual harassment and bullying.

At least 14 new complaints of a sexual nature were made to the Law Society after the summer clerk allegations blew up in the media, and it is not known whether any related to the same events (Borrisenko 2018). The *Mr X* case, mentioned earlier, may foreshadow a more open approach. The Committee took the case following an own motion investigation, and a lawyer was fined and censured after being found guilty of unsatisfactory conduct for sexually harassing two law firm employees. A document that appears to be the entire decision has been posted on the Law Society's website (*Standards Committee determination following own motion investigation of Mr X* (25 October 2018) Lawyers Standards Committee decisions (Notice of determination, ZTUVK)). His identity remains confidential.

Another recent incident involved a disciplinary investigation in which a Law Society manager mistakenly emailed very sensitive information to a person with a similar name to the intended recipient. When the mistake was discovered, the Law Society applied for a "super-injunction", which suppresses the existence of the injunction itself, as well as all details covered by it (Mau 2018). Subsequent legal challenges led to a modified order, widespread publicity, and another public outcry (Mau and Milne 2018). Minister of Justice Andrew Little said that the super-injuction was a "mis-step" by the Law Society and that it looked "like a bit of panic reaction" (Mau and Milne 2018).

Protecting consumers of legal services and maintaining public confidence are two of the three purposes of the *LCA* (s. 3(1)(a)(b)). Having as transparent a discipline system as possible serves these purposes and is particularly important now.

The critical importance of willingness to complain

People with knowledge of likely wrong-doing by lawyers must be willing to complain if a complaints-driven process like New Zealand's is to function effectively.

Reluctance to complain

Any person with knowledge of possible wrongdoing by a lawyer may (or, in some cases, must) complain about them – not just clients, but also employers, colleagues, opposing counsel, judges and others (*LCA* s. 132). Survey data on the number of people who possess strong evidence of wrongdoing and fail to make a complaint are not available, yet there is recent anecdotal evidence indicating that many hesitate to complain, at least about certain sensitive forms of wrong-doing. As discussed above, there was at least initial reluctance to complain in the case of the summer law clerks, and it is not known whether that matter was ever investigated by the Society as a consequence.

A national survey of lawyers done by the Law Society in 2018 showed that approximately one out of every five responding lawyers reported having been sexually harassed in a way contravening the Human Rights Act 1993 (Colmar Brunton 2018, p. 4). Yet, there was a marked hesitation to complain. Fewer than 1% of the lawyers who experienced legally actionable harassment reported it to the Law Society (p. 28). Not all the harassment was done by lawyers, for example 14% was reported as done by clients, but most of the harassers were the target's manager, supervisor, partner, director or senior co-worker, and thus subject to being reported to the Law Society (p. 25).

This reluctance may have been limited to the areas of sexual harassment and bullying, as they are extremely sensitive, but that is not known because other areas have not received the same level of investigation. The reluctance may have only affected lawyers, but again that is not known, because the survey only polled lawyers. Many of the explanations given by survey respondents for failing to report could apply to other people and other types of complaints, including fear of consequences for their career (49%), concern that reporting would make the situation worse (38%), and not wanting to get the offender into trouble (19%). Also mentioned were a perception that reporting would make no difference (40%); concern over an expected lack of confidentiality (30%); a lack of confidence that the Law Society could resolve the matter (15%); and not knowing who to go to or how to report the issue (17%) (Colmar Brunton 2018, p. 29). Again, these concerns are not unique to lawyers or harassment and bullying.

Mandatory reporting

The demonstrated reluctance to complain is particularly disturbing given that the professional rules for lawyers provide that those who have reasonable grounds to *suspect* that another lawyer has been guilty of misconduct are *required* to make a confidential report to the Law Society "at the earliest opportunity" (*LCA (Lawyers: Conduct and Client Care) Rules 2008* rule 2.8). This obligation applies irrespective of whether the lawyer personally observed or experienced the conduct, and covers information that the prospective reporter became aware of as a supervisor, employer, colleague or bystander (NZLS n.d.h). There is an exception for privileged – but not confidential – information. If the suspected wrongdoing is considered to be unsatisfactory conduct rather than misconduct, the lawyer may choose to report, but is under no obligation to do so (Rule 2.9).

Large percentages of the legal profession have experienced, witnessed or heard of inappropriate conduct but failed to report it to the Law Society. There may have been uncertainty at the time over whether certain conduct, for example during breaks or at social functions, counted as occurring at a time when the lawyer "is providing regulated services", as is required for the most common form of misconduct (*LCA* s. 7(1)(a)). Misconduct also covers conduct unconnected with the provision of regulated services, however, if it would justify a finding that a lawyer is not a fit and proper person, or is otherwise unsuited to engage in the practice of law (*LCA* s. 7(1)(b)(ii)). This issue has now been clarified by a Committee decision finding that sexual harassment at social events organised by a law firm (one on-site and the other off-site but with transport arranged by the firm) occurred at a time when the lawyer was providing regulated services (*Standards Committee determination following own motion investigation of Mr X* (25 October 2018) Lawyers Standards Committee decisions (Notice of determination, ZTUVK) at [32]-[33]). The lawyer in that case was found guilty of unsatisfactory conduct, so mandatory reporting would not have applied, but the boundaries between unsatisfactory conduct and misconduct are unclear. If in any doubt about whether behaviour constituted unsatisfactory conduct or misconduct, the lawyer should err on the side of filing a report.

To address these concerns, two things should be done. First, there needs to be further empirical investigation into unwillingness to complain. Significant attention has been given to lawyers' hesitation to complain about sexual violence, harassment and bullying, and useful recommendations for reform have been made (NZLS Working Group 2018). A reluctance to complain, however, is almost certainly not limited to this context. Aggrieved persons, including clients, may be deterred by the assumed stress of making a complaint and pressing it in the face of possible denial and counter-attack by the lawyer involved. They may lack trust in the willingness of the Complaints Service to be fair and hold fellow lawyers to account. Investigation of reluctance could lead to useful information such as ways to support complainants through the process, or a need to more vigorously enforce the lawyers' duty under Rule 3.4(d) to provide clients with information on complaint procedures in their practices and on the availability of the Law Society's Complaints Service.

Second, where investigation of a complaint leads to evidence that a lawyer had reasonable grounds to suspect misconduct by another and failed to report it in a timely fashion, an investigation should be triggered into the failure to report. Committees should be vigorous in pursuing and disciplining these lawyers, using own motion investigations if necessary (*LCA* s. 130(c)). The mandatory obligation to report suspected misconduct is an important part of lawyers' professional duties, and enforcement is the best way to guarantee that lawyers will honour their obligation. Failure to call out the misbehaviour of other lawyers can give rise to public perceptions of an "old boys network" and a lack of confidence in the profession's ability to self-regulate properly. This provision in the Rules must be seen to be diligently enforced to prevent these effects, and to convince practitioners that they must obey it, even in situations where that is difficult. The sole exception to this vigorous enforcement should be a discretion to exempt the target of the lawyer's misbehaviour. It would be inappropriate in many circumstances to discipline a victim who failed to make a report due to the stressful, damaging or intimidating features of another lawyer's behaviour.

Conclusion

Great trust and confidence is reposed in lawyers by clients, courts and the legal system, and an effective disciplinary system to police any breaches is vitally important. New Zealand's disciplinary regime is, in general, working well. The grounds for discipline are very broad. They include over-charging, a lack of competence, and some private behaviour as well as wrong-doing in the course of professional responsibilities. Complaints against lawyers are free and can be made by anyone. Many practitioners have been held to account by the system for their actions.

Nevertheless, some aspects of the system cause concern. While significant improvement has lessened some delays in resolving complaints, especially at the LCRO level, there is evidence that delays may be increasing in the Standards Committee Early Resolution Service. Insufficient publicity on the workings of the disciplinary system and the outcomes of cases has been noted. It is of particular concern that Committee decisions are not available online in searchable full-text format for the edification of lawyers and the public. In addition, requiring the approval of the Law Society Board before publishing the identity of a lawyer who has been censured is inappropriate and sends the wrong message to the public. The Committees, with LCRO review, should be responsible for making suppression decisions. The system also needs to be more transparent. Transparency permits accurate assessments, thus facilitating any necessary reforms, and promoting public trust and confidence in the system. Secrecy engenders distrust, and encourages the suspicion that the system is more concerned with protecting fellow practitioners and its own reputation than it is with protecting the public. Finally, people with information about wrongdoing by lawyers need to be supported in making complaints, and there needs to be vigorous enforcement of mandatory reporting requirements for lawyers.

The Law Society is conducting an extensive independent review of its structure and function which began in 2019. The Lawyers Complaints Service will be part of this review. Surveys of the profession, the report of the working group, and recent suggestions by the LCRO will all inform this review and assist with improving the disciplinary system.

Disclosure statement

No potential conflict of interest was reported by the author(s).

Funding

This work was supported by the International Institute for the Sociology of Law, Oñati, Spain.

ORCID

Selene E. Mize http://orcid.org/0000-0002-6981-1552

References

ABA Standing Committee on Professional Regulation. (2019) 2017 Survey on Lawyer Discipline Systems. Available at: https://www.americanbar.org/content/dam/aba/administrative/professional_responsibility/2017sold-results.pdf, accessed 1 July 2020.

Bazley, M. (2018) Independent review of Russell McVeagh. Available at: https://www.russellmcveagh.com/getmedia/cc682d64-46a1-40e3-987b-cd82223bea24/Independent-Review-of-Russell-McVeagh-2018.pdf/, accessed 1 July 2020.

Borissenko, S. (2018) Did the Law Society do enough?, *Newsroom*, 11 June. Available at: https://www.newsroom.co.nz/2018/06/05/112498/did-the-law-society-do-enough, accessed 1 July 2020.

Borissenko, S. & Reid, M. (2018) The summer interns and the law firm, *Newsroom*, 14 February. Available at: https://www.newsroom.co.nz/2018/02/14/88663/the-summer-interns-and-the-law-firm, accessed 1 July 2020.

Clarkson, D. (n.d.a) *Annual report of the New Zealand Lawyers and Conveyancers Disciplinary Tribunal for the 12 months ended 30 June 2018*. Available at: https://www.justice.govt.nz/assets/Documents/Publications/2018-LCDT-annual-report.pdf, accessed 1 July 2020.

Clarkson, D. (n.d.b) *New Zealand Lawyers and Conveyancers Disciplinary Tribunal annual report for the 12 months ended 30 June 2017*. Available at: https://www.justice.govt.nz/assets/Documents/Publications/2017-lcdt-annual-report.pdf, accessed 1 July 2020.

Clarkson, D. (n.d.c) *New Zealand Lawyers and Conveyancers Disciplinary Tribunal annual report for the 12 months ended 30 June 2016*. Available at: https://www.justice.govt.nz/assets/Documents/Publications/2015-2016-lcdt-annual-report.pdf, accessed 1 July 2020.

Clarkson, D. (n.d.d) *New Zealand Lawyers and Conveyancers Disciplinary Tribunal annual report for the 12 months ended 30 June 2015*. Available at: https://www.justice.govt.nz/assets/Documents/Publications/LCDT-2015-annual-report.pdf, accessed 1 July 2020.

Clarkson, D. (n.d.e) *New Zealand Lawyers and Conveyancers Disciplinary Tribunal annual report for the 12 months ended 30 June 2014*. Available at: https://www.justice.govt.nz/assets/Documents/Publications/LCDT-2014-annual-report.pdf, accessed 1 July 2020.

Clarkson, D. (n.d.f) *New Zealand Lawyers and Conveyancers Disciplinary Tribunal annual report for the 12 months ended 30 June 2013*. Available at: https://www.justice.govt.nz/assets/Documents/Publications/LCDT-2013-annual-report.pdf, accessed 1 July 2020.

Clarkson, D. (n.d.g) *New Zealand Lawyers and Conveyancers Disciplinary Tribunal annual report for the 12 months ended 30 June 2012*. Available at: https://www.justice.govt.nz/assets/Documents/Publications/LCDT-Annual-Report-2012.pdf, accessed 1 July 2020.

Colmar Brunton. (2018) *Workplace environment survey: prepared for the New Zealand Law Society*, 28 May. Available at: https://www.lawsociety.org.nz/__data/assets/pdf_file/0009/122679/Report-28-May-2018.pdf, accessed 1 July 2020.

Gay, E. (2019) Name suppression: how the uniquely kiwi 'hush hush policy' became law and morphed over a century. *Stuff*, 3 November. Available at: https://www.stuff.co.nz/national/crime/117058919/name-suppression-how-the-uniquely-kiwi-hush-hush-policy-became-law-and-morphed-over-a-century, accessed 1 July 2020.

Hancock, F., Reid, M. & Borissenko, S. (2018) Why wasn't the Law Society told? *Newsroom*, 24 February. Available at: https://www.newsroom.co.nz/2018/02/21/90108/why-wasnt-the-law-society-told#, accessed 1 July 2020.

Lawyers Complaints Service. (2018) Complaint resolution summaries. *LawTalk* 916, April, pp. 72–74.

LCRO. (n.d.a) *Annual report of the Legal Complaints Review Officer for the 12 months ended 30 June 2019*. Available at: https://www.justice.govt.nz/assets/Documents/Publications/2019-LCRO-Annual-report.pdf, accessed 1 July 2020.

LCRO. (n.d.b) *Annual report of the Legal Complaints Review Officer for the 12 months ended 30 June 2018*. Available at: https://www.justice.govt.nz/assets/Documents/Publications/2018-LCRO-Annual-Report.pdf, accessed 1 July 2020.

LCRO. (n.d.c) *Report of the Legal Complaints Review Officer for the 11 months ended 30 June 2009*. Available at: https://www.justice.govt.nz/assets/Documents/Publications/Annual-report-Period-ending-30-June-2009.pdf, accessed 1 July 2020.

LCRO. (n.d.d) *Annual report of the Legal Complaints Review Officer for the 12 months ended 30 June 2017*. Available at: https://www.justice.govt.nz/assets/Documents/Publications/LCRO-Annual-Report-2017.pdf, accessed 1 July 2020.

LCRO. (n.d.e) *Annual report of the Legal Complaints Review Officer for the 12 months ended 30 June 2015*. Available at: https://www.justice.govt.nz/assets/Documents/Publications/LCRO-2015-annual-report.pdf, accessed 1 July 2020.

LCRO. (n.d.f) *Report of the Legal Complaints Review Officer for the 12 months ended 30 June 2010*. Available at: https://www.justice.govt.nz/assets/Documents/Publications/Annual-Report-period-ending-30-June-2010.pdf, accessed 1 July 2020.

LCRO. (n.d.g) *Report of the Legal Complaints Review Officer for the 12 months ended 30 June 2011*. Available at: https://www.justice.govt.nz/assets/Documents/Publications/Annual-Report-period-ending-30-June-2011.pdf, accessed 1 July 2020.

LCRO. (n.d.h) *Annual report of the Legal Complaints Review Officer for the 12 months ended 30 June 2013*. Available at: https://www.justice.govt.nz/assets/Documents/Publications/LCRO-2013-annual-report.pdf, accessed 1 July 2020.

LCRO. (n.d.i) *Report of the Legal Complaints Review Officer for the 12 months ended 30 June 2012*. Available at: https://www.justice.govt.nz/assets/Documents/Publications/Annual-Report-period-ending-30-June-2012.pdf, accessed 1 July 2020.

LCRO. (n.d.j) *Annual report of the Legal Complaints Review Officer for the 12 months ended 30 June 2014*. Available at: https://www.justice.govt.nz/assets/Documents/Publications/LCRO-2014-annual-report.pdf, accessed 1 July 2020.

LCRO. (n.d.k) *Annual report of the Legal Complaints Review Officer for the 12 months ended 30 June 2016*. Available at: https://www.justice.govt.nz/assets/Documents/Publications/LCRO-2016-annual-report.pdf, accessed 1 July 2020.

Logan, A. (2018) Creating a just culture. *LawTalk* 920, August, p. 7.

Mau, A. (2018) Justice Minister demands explanation of super-injunction hiding sexual harassment. *Sunday Star Times*, 3 August. Available at: https://www.stuff.co.nz/national/106005111/justice-minister-demands-explanation-of-superinjunction-hiding-sexual-harassment, accessed 1 July 2020.

Mau, A. & Milne, J. (2018) Law Society super-injunction overturned, allowing disclosure of sexual harassment case. *Sunday Star Times*, 3 August. Available at: https://www.stuff.co.

nz/national/105975362/law-society-superinjunction-overturned-allowing-disclosure-of-sexual-harassment-case?rm=m, accessed 1 July 2020.

Mize, S. (2018) New Zealand: finding the balance between self-regulation and government oversight', in: A. Boon (Ed) *International Perspectives on the Regulation of Lawyers and Legal Services* (Oxford, Hart Publishing), pp. 115–138.

NZLS. (n.d.a) *Annual report for the year to 30 June 2019*. Available at: https://www.lawsociety.org.nz/__data/assets/pdf_file/0020/144632/2018-19-regulatory-report.pdf, accessed 1 July 2020.

NZLS. (n.d.b) *Annual report for the year to 30 June 2018*. Available at: https://www.lawsociety.org.nz/__data/assets/pdf_file/0017/132092/2018-Annual-Report.pdf, accessed 1 July 2020.

NZLS. (n.d.c) *Lawyers Complaints Service*. Available at: http://www.lawsociety.org.nz/for-the-community/lawyers-complaints-service, accessed 1 July 2020.

NZLS. (n.d.d) *Report on regulatory activities for the year to 30 June 2017*. Available at: https://www.lawsociety.org.nz/__data/assets/pdf_file/0017/118214/2016-17-regulatory-report.pdf, accessed 1 July 2020.

NZLS. (n.d.e) *Report on regulatory activities for the year to 30 June 2016*. Available at: https://www.lawsociety.org.nz/__data/assets/pdf_file/0006/107565/2016-Regulatory-Report.pdf, accessed 1 July 2020.

NZLS. (n.d.f) *Report on the exercise of regulatory functions and powers for the year to 30 June 2015*. Available at: https://www.lawsociety.org.nz/__data/assets/pdf_file/0010/96913/2015-NZLS-Regulatory-Annual-Report-2.pdf, accessed 1 July 2020.

NZLS. (n.d.g) *Report on the exercise of regulatory functions and powers for the year to 30 June 2014*. Available at: https://www.lawsociety.org.nz/__data/assets/pdf_file/0003/85242/NZLS-2014-Regulatory-Report-WEB.pdf, accessed 1 July 2020.

NZLS. (n.d.h) *Reporting unacceptable conduct*. Available at: https://www.lawsociety.org.nz/for-lawyers/confidential-report, accessed 1 July 2020.

NZLS. (2017) *Lawyers Standards Committee decisions*, 10 July. Available at: https://www.lawsociety.org.nz/for-the-community/lawyers-standards-committee-decisions, accessed 1 July 2020. [While this page is dated July 2017, it has clearly been updated since then.].

NZLS. (2018) *Law Society plans changes to regulatory process for lawyers accused of inappropriate behaviour*, 17 December. Available at: https://www.lawsociety.org.nz/news-and-communications/news/law-society-plans-changes-to-regulatory-process-for-lawyers-accused-of-inappropriate-behaviour, accessed 1 July 2020.

NZLS. (2019) *NZ Law Society to commission comprehensive review*, 23 October. Available at: https://www.lawsociety.org.nz/news-and-communications/news/nz-law-society-to-commission-comprehensive-review, accessed 1 July 2020.

NZLS Working Group. (2018) *Report*, 8 February. Available at: https://www.lawsociety.org.nz/__data/assets/pdf_file/0007/129922/Report-of-the-NZLS-Working-Group-December-2018.pdf, accessed 1 July 2020.

NZ Ministry of Justice. (n.d.) *Legal Complaints Review Officer decisions*. Available at: https://www.justice.govt.nz/tribunals/lawyers-and-conveyancers/lcro/lcro-decisions/?Filter_Jurisdiction=29, accessed 1 July 2020.

Scragg, R. (2018) *The Ethical Lawyer: Legal Ethics and Professional Responsibility* (Wellington, Thomson Reuters.

Solicitors Disciplinary Tribunal. (2018) *Annual Report 1 January-31 December 2018*. Available at: https://www.solicitorstribunal.org.uk/sites/default/files-sdt/ANNUAL%20REPORT%202018.pdf, accessed 1 July 2020.

The nature of the disciplinary system over Myanmar lawyers: differences from international standards and implications for international legal transplants

Jonathan Liljeblad

ABSTRACT

International organizations such as the International Bar Association (IBA), International Commission of Jurists (ICJ), and United Nations (UN) have been engaged in efforts to reform Myanmar's laws regarding the legal profession as part of larger rule-of-law initiatives in the country. Part of such efforts are strategies to change professional conduct rules to match international practices in the regulation of lawyers. The present analysis focuses on the disciplinary mechanisms for lawyers in Myanmar. The analysis seeks to determine the extent to which Myanmar's existing disciplinary mechanisms for lawyers deviate from international standards held by the IBA, ICJ, and UN. The analysis argues that the structural nature of Myanmar's disciplinary system renders it incapable of meeting international expectations because it sustains British colonial laws that centralized power over lawyers underneath institutions of the state. The analysis identifies the significance of these deviations for international legal transplant efforts.

Introduction

From 2014–2016, the International Bar Association (IBA) Human Rights Initiative (IBAHRI) worked to promote the idea of an independent national bar association in Myanmar, the country formerly known as Burma. The project culminated in the formation of the Independent Lawyers' Association of Myanmar (ILAM), which seeks to be a nation-wide organization for the Myanmar legal profession operating outside the control of the Myanmar state (IBA 2015b). As a product of the IBAHRI, ILAM is an outcome of IBA efforts reflective of the IBA's conceptions regarding the legal profession. To the extent that the creation of ILAM involves IBA perspectives, ILAM provides a case study exemplifying an attempted transmission of international expectations for an independent national bar association into a domestic context.

Among the IBA's conceptions regarding the legal profession are elements addressing disciplinary systems for lawyers. IBA standards for the independence of lawyers expect lawyer associations to have the authority separate from the state to adopt professional codes of conduct, enforce compliance, and administer discipline over association members (IBA 1990). Such notions imply that 1) under the IBA issues of lawyer discipline should be addressed outside the state and 2) ILAM should gain some role in the disciplining of Myanmar lawyers if it is to fulfill IBA standards for an independent bar. In addition, such notions also suggest that the extent to which the disciplinary system for Myanmar lawyers lies with an authority outside the state offers some indication of the degree to which Myanmar's legal system aligns with international expectations, and thereby provides some direction as to the nature of reforms that are necessary to make it so.

The present study focuses on assessing Myanmar's disciplinary system for lawyers relative to international expectations. Specifically, the analysis in subsequent sections compares the disciplinary system for lawyers in Myanmar against the standards of the IBA, with reference to comparable standards of the International Commission of Jurists (ICJ) and the United Nations (UN) for context. The analysis argues that the structural nature of Myanmar's system renders it incapable of meeting IBA expectations because it sustains British colonial laws that centralized power over lawyers underneath institutions of the state. The persistence of such a power structure in Myanmar's post-independence history, attendant with its abuse of lawyers during Myanmar's authoritarian regimes, were among the motivations driving IBAHRI efforts for an independent bar association (IBA 2012a). While it may be axiomatic that aspirations for the independence of lawyers requires a discontinuation of colonial-era laws, the analysis goes further to determine what specific types of changes in such laws are necessary to fulfill IBA expectations regarding the disciplining of lawyers. The discussion begins with a review of theory that frames the analysis, followed by a review of the IBAHRI's work that led to ILAM. The analysis then delineates the disciplinary system for lawyers in Myanmar and proceeds to study how it deviates from the IBA, ICJ, and UN standards. The discussion draws implications for the theoretical literature as well as ongoing international aid efforts to promote an independent legal profession in Myanmar. The conclusion then notes future directions for research.

Methodologically, the analysis in the following sections is part of an ongoing research project on the experiences of ILAM. Due to the sensitive nature of ongoing negotiations between ILAM and the Myanmar state to reform Myanmar's legal system, relevant parties declined interviews to discuss potential plans to change the disciplinary system. As a result, the scope of study is focused on the current disciplinary system prescribed by existing Myanmar laws and its contrast with international standards. The goal is that such descriptive analysis serves to illuminate understanding of the challenges facing legal reforms in Myanmar and thereby informs prescriptive analysis to unpack the types of actions that can facilitate efforts to bring Myanmar's legal system into greater alignment with international expectations.

Theory

It is possible to understand the work of the IBAHRI to produce ILAM as a legal transplant, with ILAM being the outcome of a project to introduce the idea of an international bar association into Myanmar in accordance with international standards held by the IBA. The concept of a legal transplant is summarized by Andrew Harding, who frames the idea between the perspectives of Alan Watson and Pierre Legrand, with Watson treating legal concepts as autonomous from context and so readily transferable across different locations while LeGrand views legal concepts as unique to each context and hence wholly non-transferable from one place to another (Harding 2019; Legrand 1997; Watson 1993). The discourse on legal transplants, however, predates both Watson and Legrand. For example, John Cairns finds that the term "transplants" in legal scholarship occurs as early as 1927 in a speech to the International Academy of Comparative Law by Frederick P. Walton in which he described cases where countries adopted foreign legal systems in lieu of their own legal heritage (Cairns 2013; Walton 1927). In addition, Cairns finds examples from the 1930s in the works of R.W. Lee on the spread of Roman-Dutch law to European colonies, Hermann Mannheim's study on the European adoption of juries in criminal trials from England, and Henri Levy Ullmann's observation of Turkey's legal development (Cairns 2013: 694). The metaphor of transplantats also appears in the 1950s, with examples including B.A. Watley's report on the 1950 Rome UNIDROIT conference (Watley 1950) and C.J. Hamson's summary of the International 1955 Istanbul meeting for the Committee on Comparative Law (Hamson 1956). The use of the term persisted and grew in subsequent decades, appearing in Alan Watson's seminal book on *Legal Transplants* (Watson 1993), Otto Kahn-Freund's Chorley Lecture of 1973 (Freedland 2004), John Beckstrom's work on the transplantation of legal systems from 1973 (Beckstrom 1973), and Jean Rivero's metaphor of medical organ transplants to describe local imitation of foreign legal models from 1980 (Rivero 1980).

In conceptualizing legal transplants, there are a range of approaches that help to clarify its implications. For example, Anna Dolidze describes legal transplants as being horizontal, with transnational diffusion of ideas between states, or vertical, with diffusion either going up from domestic law to international law or diffused down from international law to domestic law (Dolidze 2016). An alternative perspective is posed by John Gillespie, who uses discourse analysis to interpret legal transplants through the exploration of power structures and individual agency in lawmaking processes (Gillespie 2008). Also useful is Jonathan Miller's adoption of a typology that classifies legal transplants as involving cases of 1) cost-saving, where a drafter of a law tries to save time and costs in experimentation by using a foreign solution; 2) externally-dictated, where dominant foreign actors impose the adoption of foreign legal models in a country; 3) entrepreneurial, where domestic actors adopt foreign legal ideas into their own country; or 4) legitimacy-generating, where domestic actors use prestigious foreign legal ideas to bolster their own domestic legitimacy (Miller 2003). In contrast, John Wise sees the term "transplant" as implying a reductionist dichotomy of internal versus external, and favors instead terms like "borrowing," "circulation," and "diffusion" that offer a more accurate description of the movements of ideas in transnational cultural networks (Wise 1990). John Gillespie, Sally Low, and Penelope Nicholson assert the need for development actors to heed local experiences, noting that the success or failure of legal transfers is a function of social demand in recipient countries (Nicholson & Low 2013; Nicholson & Gillespie 2012).

With respect to the tensions between Watson and Legrand, there is some utility in referencing Otto Kahn-Freund's notion of a spectrum encompassing legal institutions that are mechanical in the sense of being insulated from culture versus legal institutions that are organic in the sense of being culturally embedded (Cairns 2013: 643-645; Kahn-Freund 1978: 298; Teubner 1998). Otto Kahn-Freund postulated that more mechanical legal institutions are relatively easy to transfer between cultures while organic ones are more difficult to transfer to alien cultures. Such thinking accommodates Watson and Legrand, in that Watson's position accepts the existence of legal transplants and Legrand's position considers it impractical or inappropriate. Watson and Legrand would exist as the polar extremes in Kahn-Freund's spectrum, leaving the space in between them as a continuum of varying perspectives on legal transplants. Scholars who would lie within the continuum include examples like Melissa Crouch and David Nelken, who see legal transplants as conceptually useful in understanding the transnational spread of legal ideas so long as they are qualified by some consideration of local context (Crouch 2013; Nelken 2002). Another example is Gunther Teubner, who differs from Crouch and Nelken in exercising a dialectical approach that interprets a legal transplant as affecting change within a new context but also being subject to change by the forces within it (Teubner 1998). Teubner goes beyond the Watson-Legrand dichotomy of integration or repulsion of legal ideas across cultures, and instead adopts the idea of legal irritants that cause unexpected consequences via an "evolutionary dynamic in which the external rule's meaning will be reconstructed and the internal context will undergo fundamental change" (Teubner 1998: 12). Teubner conceives of legal irritants as operating in two ways: 1) a legal transformation, where a legal idea is recontextualized by new conditions but may still be recognizable even though its legal interpretation changes from the original; and 2) a social transformation, where the recognition of a legal idea will cause changes in a social system even as the idea is reconstructed by the system. Teubner goes further to assert that these two processes are inter-connected via a "circular co-evolutionary dynamic" of "mutual irritations" upon each other that ultimately changes the content of the legal idea (Teubner 1998: 28).

The varying conceptualizations of legal transplants offer a means of understanding the IBAHRI's work for an independent national bar association in Myanmar, framing it in general terms as a transmission of international norms represented by the IBA to the domestic context of Myanmar. In which case, the experiences associated with the formation of ILAM provide some grounds for reflection about the nature of legal transplantation. In particular, with respect to the topic of disciplinary systems for lawyers, the issues posed by ILAM's role in lawyer discipline serves as a means of assessing the status of Myanmar legal reforms against international expectations and identifying the changes necessary to bring them into alignment with each other.

Background – status of international efforts for an international legal profession

The idea of an independent bar association for Myanmar was undertaken by the IBA as an IBAHRI project that lasted from 2014–2016. The IBAHRI for Myanmar arose in the wake of fact-finding missions by the IBA and the International Commission of Jurists (ICJ) which observed that Myanmar's legal profession suffered from a lack of independence (IBA 2012a; ICJ 2013). The IBA mission report claimed that over a period of two decades there were more than 1000 cases involving potential abuses of Myanmar's disciplinary system against lawyers critical of the government (IBA 2012a: 64). The ICJ could not confirm exact figures, but its mission noted a persistence of cases wherein the disciplinary system was used to harass lawyers for political purposes (ICJ 2013: 24-25). The IBA's 2012 fact-finding mission led to a subsequent 2013 panel discussion on rule-of-law in the country and an additional 2013 scoping mission on potential reforms, after which the IBA committed itself to promoting an independent national bar association in Myanmar (IBA 2013b; IBA 2012a; IBA 2012b). During its time, the IBAHRI program worked to 1) nurture domestic Myanmar support for a national bar association, 2) establish a national bar association as a legally registered entity, and 3) promote reforms that would allow the national bar association to operate independent of the Myanmar state (IBA 2015b; IBA 2013a).

In pursuing the goal of an independent national bar association, the IBAHRI hosted a series of workshops and seminars in partnership with the Myanmar Parliament's Committee on Law and Tranquility, which was led by its Chair Daw Aung San Suu Kyi. The workshops and seminars addressing international standards for bar associations (IBA 2016a; IBA 2014f), recommendations on reform for Myanmar's legal profession (IBA 2014e; IBA 2014f), the construction of a steering committee and formal statement to create an independent national bar association (IBA 2014d), and a comparative review of laws from other countries with discussions on enacting Myanmar legislation more consistent with international standards for regulation of lawyers (IBA 2014a;

IBA 2014b). In addition, the IBAHRI supported meetings to draft a constitution (IBA 2014c), a March 2015 general assembly to endorse a draft constitution (IBA 2015a), and further workshops in the various states and administrative regions of Myanmar to prepare the first elections under the constitution (IBA 2015a). The product of such efforts was the Independent Lawyers' Association of Myanmar (ILAM), which held its first elections in September 2015 (IBA 2015a), and with the IBA convened an inaugural meeting in January 2016 (IBA 2016b). ILAM became a legally registered entity in November 2016 (ILAM 2017), effectively serving as the culmination of the IBAHRI's three-year program in Myanmar.

Normatively, the IBAHRI's work to produce ILAM followed the IBA's expectations for the legal profession. The IBA's expectations are articulated in its 1990 Standards for the Independence of the Legal Profession (IBA Standards) (IBA 1990), which in reference to the nature of lawyer disciplinary systems presents the following principles:

- Principle 6: Lawyers should act freely, diligently, and fearlessly in accordance with the legitimate interest of the client & without any inhibition or pressure from the authorities or the public
- Principle 8: No penal, civil, administrative, economic, or other sanctions or harassment for legitimately representing client
- Principles 21-24: Lawyers' associations shall adopt & enforce professional code of conduct, disciplinary proceedings shall follow principles of natural justice, disciplinary proceedings should in first instance be conducted by disciplinary committee of lawyers' association (IBA 1990: Principles 6, 8, 21-24)

The IBA's position regarding norms for lawyer discipline are not unique, in that they parallel positions held by the ICJ and UN. With respect to the independence of lawyers, the ICJ's *Practitioners' Guide No. 1 – Independence of Judges, Lawyers, and Prosecutors* quotes the UN Basic Principles on the Roles of Lawyers 1990 (UN Basic Principles), which reads that "adequate protection of the human rights and fundamental freedoms to which all persons are entitled … requires that all persons have effective access to legal services provided by an independent legal profession" (ICJ 2004; UN Basic Principles 1990). For its part, the UN Basic Principles also directs governments to ensure that lawyers do not "suffer or be threatened with prosecution or sanctions for any action" that follows professional duties, standards, or ethics (UN Basic Principles 1990: Principle 16). In relation to the Myanmar, the principle expects the government to not subject lawyers to punishment for actions in the course of their professional duties. In addition, the UN Basic Principles states that "Lawyers are entitled to form and join self-governing professional associations" for purposes of advancing their interests, continuing legal education, and integrity (UN Basic Principles 1990: Principle 24), and so encompasses the concept of a national bar association which represents Myanmar lawyers and is independent of control from the Myanmar government.

The IBAHRI's work to produce ILAM is consistent with Gunther Teubner's conception of legal transplants, in that the IBAHRI constituted a foreign irritant into Myanmar's domestic legal space and the IBAHRI's efforts to form ILAM represented a transnational conveyance of IBA expectations regarding an independent national bar association into Myanmar (Liljeblad 2019). To the extent that IBA expectations encompassed ideas about lawyer discipline, ILAM's ongoing position in Myanmar's system for disciplining lawyers provides a means of evaluating the current status of Myanmar's legal reforms against international norms. Specifically, it allows assessment of the extent to which Myanmar deviates from international standards of lawyer discipline and thereby enables identification of the changes needed to bring Myanmar into greater alignment with international expectations regarding disciplinary systems for lawyers.

Disciplinary system for Myanmar lawyers

In evaluating the IBAHRI's work with respect to the topic of lawyer discipline in Myanmar, it is useful to place the IBAHRI project within the history of Myanmar's constraints upon the independence of the country's legal profession (Crouch 2014; IBA 2012a; ICJ 2013; Kham 2014). The constraints, which extend from Myanmar's past as British colonial Burma, continue to operate against the two categories of lawyers in Myanmar: pleaders, who are licensed to practice in civil and criminal matters in district and township courts, and advocates, who are licensed to practice in all courts including the Supreme Court (Bar Council Act 1929; Courts Manual 1999; Legal Practitioners Act 1879; Kham 2014). Laws for both originate in British colonial Burma. Pleaders were subject to the Legal Practitioners Act of 1879 (based on the India Act XVIII 1879), which gave authority for regulation, licensing, and discipline to the High Court (Legal Practitioners Act 1879: Sect. 6 & 607), and advocates were subject to the Bar Council Act of 1929 (based on the India Act XXXVIII of 1926), which placed authority over rules, licenses, and discipline in the High Court but makes the High Court subject to the authority of the Bar Council (Bar Council Act 1929: Sect. 25, 8-9, 14-16; Courts Manual 1999: Part 1, Sect. 1-2). The Bar Council was originally composed of fifteen members chaired by the Attorney General and filled with four nominees from the High Court and ten members elected by practicing advocates (Bar Council Act 1929). This arrangement continued into post-independence through much of the military era, with the Supreme Court of Myanmar holding the place of the High Court of British colonial Burma and the the Bar Council being amended in 1989 to have eleven members comprised of the Attorney General as Chair, Deputy Attorney General as Vice-Chair, the Director-General of the Attorney General's Office as Secretary, a Supreme Court Judge nominated by the Chief Justice, the Director-General of the Supreme Court, and six advocates chosen by the Supreme Court (Bar Council Act Amendment 1989; Courts Manual 1999). Myanmar's judicial system places the High Court at the administrative state or region level and the Supreme Court at the national level (Kham 2014), so the Bar Council Act Amendment of 1989 served to centralize control over the country's lawyers within national state authority. More recently, in June 2019 the Myanmar Parliament passed the Bar Council Act Amendment of 2019, which modifies the Bar Council with a composition of the Attorney General, Deputy Attorney General, two Supreme Court justices selected by the Chief Justice, and eleven members elected by the country's advocates (Bar Council Act Amendment 2019). The Bar Council Act Amendment of 2019, however, retains the existing disciplinary system for Myanmar lawyers (Bar Council Act Amendment 2019).

It should be noted that there are local bar associations entirely separate from the Myanmar state, with examples including the Yangon Bar Association, Mandalay Bar Association, and Mon Bar Association. These entities, however, have never held powers to regulate the legal profession and were denied legal registration when the State Law and Order Restoration Council (SLORC) seized power (IBA 2012a; ICJ 2013). A number of these entities continue to exist, but they do so as local bar associations without the power to regulate the legal profession for the country, and hence fall short of the ideal for an independent national bar association.

The disciplinary system differs between advocates and pleaders. To begin, the Bar Council Act of 1929 (Bar Council Act) prescribes the mechanism for discipline of advocates, with the Bar Council holding authority to issue disciplinary rules and the High Court (now Supreme Court) having the power to hold hearings (Bar Council Act 1929: Sect. 10 & 15). Procedurally, the process of discipline begins when a complaint alleging misconduct by an advocate is submitted to the Supreme Court, which has the options to reject the complaint, refer it to the Bar Council for formal inquiry, or consult with the Bar Council to refer the case to a district court (Bar Council Act 1929: Sect. 10). The Bar Council, if it accepts a case for inquiry, then forms a tribunal to conduct the inquiry, with membership ranging from three to five members of the Bar Council appointed by the Chief Justice of the Supreme Court (Bar Council Act 1929: Sect 11). The Bar Council Act allows the Supreme Court to set the rules of inquiry for both Bar Council tribunals and district courts (Bar Council Act 1929: Sect. 12). In addition, however, the Bar Council Act specifies that each inquiry is considered to be a judicial proceeding under the Myanmar Penal Code, with evidentiary rules following the Evidence Act (Bar Council Act 1929: Sect. 13). Findings from a tribunal are returned to the Bar Council which relays them to the Supreme Court, and findings from a district court are sent directly to the Supreme Court with copies sent to the Bar Council (Bar Council Act 1929: Sect. 12). Upon receipt of inquiry findings, the Supreme Court conducts a formal hearing involving the accused advocate, Bar Council, and Attorney General (Bar Council Act 1929: Sect. 12). The hearing concludes with the Supreme Court either issuing final orders in the case or referring it back for further inquiry (Bar Council Act: Sect. 12). The disciplinary system was retained by the Bar Council Amendment Act of 2019 (Bar Council Act Amendment of 2019). A flowchart summarizing the above procedures is presented in Figure 1 below.

In contrast to advocates, the disciplinary system for pleaders is contained in the Legal Practitioners Act of 1879 (Legal Practitioners Act). The Legal Practitioners Act grants the High Court (now the Supreme Court) the power to make rules regarding discipline of pleaders (Legal Practitioners Act 1879: Ch. 3, Sect. 6). Issuance of certificates to practice as pleaders are issued by the Supreme Court, but renewals of certificates are conducted by the district court having jurisdiction over a pleader's geographic area of practice (Legal Practitioners Act 1879: Ch. 3, Sect. 7). In cases where a pleader has received a criminal conviction, the Supreme Court has the authority to suspend the certificate or dismiss the convicted pleader from practice (Legal Practitioners Act 1879: Ch. 3, Sect 12). With respect to cases of alleged misconduct, the disciplinary system commences with the submission of allegations to the Supreme Court, after which the court provides the accused pleader with a copy and notice of the charges, receives evidence from the accusers and the accused pleader, and then holds a hearing to adjudicate the case (Legal Practitioners Act 1879: Ch. 3, Sect. 14). The Supreme Court can suspend or dismiss a pleader for taking instructions in a case from anyone other than the client or agent of the client, engaging in fraudulent or grossly improper conduct, tendering or consenting to retention from fees involving gratification in exchange for

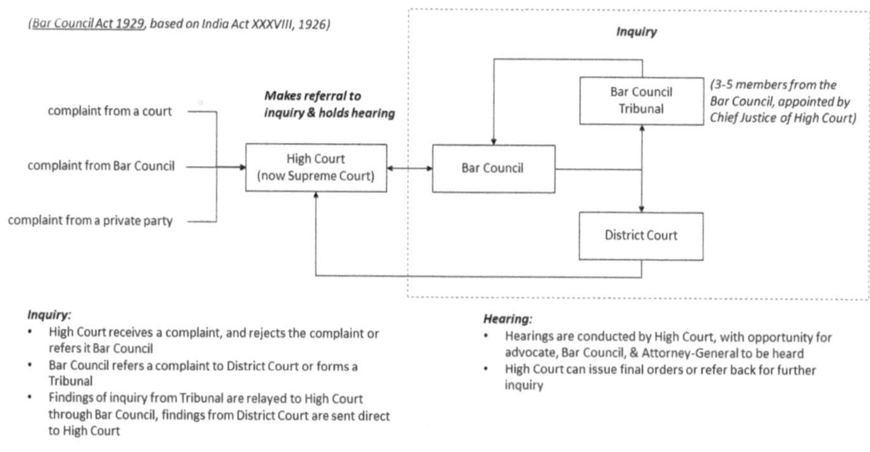

Figure 1. Disciplinary procedures for advocates.

gaining employment, directly or indirectly procuring or attempting to procure employment through a person receiving compensation for such employment, accepts employment in legal business through a tout, or any other reasonable cause (Legal Practitioners Act 1879: Ch. 3, Sect. 13). In addition to suspension or dismissal, the Supreme Court can also issue fines or jail for failure to pay such fines (Legal Practitioners Act 1879: Ch. 7). A flowchart summarizing the above procedures is presented in Figure 2 below.

Myanmar's disciplinary system and international standards

The preceding discussion on the disciplinary system for advocates and pleaders yields some issues when measured against international standards used to frame the analysis. In particular, the review of the above mechanisms reveal areas where they fall short of the norms set by the ICJ, UN, and IBA. The deviation between Myanmar and such international expectations are addressed individually below.

IBA

Myanmar struggles with respect to a number of the norms posed by the IBA. To begin, the IBA Standards declare that lawyers' associations should be responsible for adopting and enforcing codes of conduct and that in the first instance all cases involving allegations of misconduct should be addressed by disciplinary committees held by lawyers' associations (IBA 1990: Principles 21-24). The IBA Standards specify that the lawyers' associations should be independent self-governing entities (IBA 1990: Principle 17). ILAM operates as a self-governing organization and is independent of the Myanmar state, and as such is able to set its own expectations for lawyer conduct. But it does not have legal authority to discipline lawyers. Rather, the Attorney General's Office issues a national lawyer code of conduct in the form of its *Ethical Principles of Lawyers and Legal Practitioners* (UAGO 2010). Further, with respect to dealing with

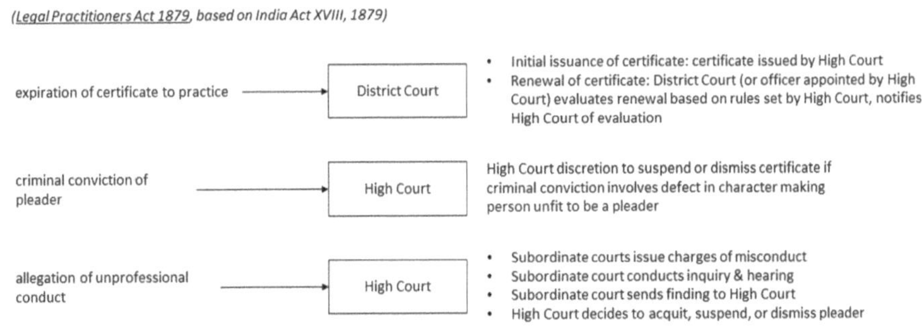

Figure 2. Disciplinary procedures for pleaders.

allegations of misconduct, the preceding sections show that the disciplinary mechanisms for both advocates and pleaders place powers over rules and procedures within the Supreme Court and so reserve the processing of cases under the authority of the Myanmar state.

The nature of the procedures themselves are also problematic, in that they directly involve entities of the state. The IBA's *International Principles on Conduct for the Legal Profession* (IBA Principles) comment that the process for discipline should be "organized and carried out in a manner that guarantees that administration of the legal profession is free from undue or improper influence, whether governmental, by the courts or otherwise" (IBA 2011: 13). The previous sections, however, identify the procedures for advocates and pleaders and demonstrate the role played by the Bar Council and the courts in the evaluation and punishment of lawyer misconduct cases. While six out of eleven members of the Bar Council are advocates, they are still chosen by the Supreme Court and so are still under control by the Myanmar state. As a result, the presence of the Myanmar state in lawyer disciplinary mechanisms is pervasive. There is a persistent likelihood that such a presence poses an undue influence, in that the history of the Myanmar state towards its legal system (Cheesman & San 2014; Crouch 2014) offers little guarantee that the state will not use its role to affect the independence of the country's advocates or pleaders.

ICJ & UN

The ICJ draws upon the UN Basic Principles, and so for purposes of organization it is possible to treat them as proffering the same types of norms. In some ways, relative to the IBA Myanmar's system enjoys greater alignment with the parameters of the ICJ and UN. For example, the UN Basic Principles state that disciplinary proceedings shall be subject to independent judicial review. For both advocates and pleaders, the mechanisms of discipline are conducted by the courts, which under Myanmar's Union Judiciary Law of 2010 and its 2008 Constitution are expected to "administer justice independently according to law" (Myanmar Constitution 2008; Union Judiciary Law 2010). In other ways, however, the system prescribed by the Bar Council Act and Legal Practitioner's Act crosses the ICJ-UN norms. Specifically, the UN Basic Principles require that "all disciplinary proceedings shall be determined in accordance with the code of professional conduct and other recognized standards and ethics of the legal profession" (UN Basic Principles 1990: Principle 29). The Attorney General Office's *Ethical Principles of Lawyers and Legal Practitioners* (Union Attorney General 2010) includes declarations that lawyers should place societal interest over self-interest (Union Attorney General 2010: Ch. 2, Para. 106), preserve justice by the courts (Union Attorney General 2010: Ch. 2, Para. 110), hold a duty of loyalty to the judiciary (Union Attorney General

2010: Ch. 2, Para. 119), and hold a duty to obey the courts and support the success of the judiciary (Union Attorney General 2010: Ch. 2, Para. 120). In effect, Myanmar ethics rules subordinate lawyers to courts, which are a state entities, and thereby subjugate lawyers to the authority of the state. Myanmar's legal ethics are consistent with its disciplinary system for advocates and pleaders, which exercises mechanisms with proceedings directed by the Supreme Court and so similarly supports the relegation of Myanmar lawyers to state control. Such logic in Myanmar's legal system works against elements of the UN Basic Principles which recognize that lawyers "are entitled to form and join self-governing professional associations" (UN Basic Principles 1990: Principle 24). State control of Myanmar lawyers contradicts the ability of a professional association such as ILAM to be truly self-governing, in that the ethical strictures and procedural mechanisms that maintain state authority for discipline collectively pressure lawyers to ultimately defer to the state rather than any professional association.

Implications for international efforts and theory

The nature of Myanmar's disciplinary system for lawyers has implications for both international efforts to promote an independent bar association in the country as well as for the theoretical literature on legal transplants. With respect to international efforts, the preceding sections suggest that the installation of a national professional organization that meets international standards for an independent bar association is a project with a scope exceeding the IBA's work on behalf of ILAM. Through its IBAHRI program in Myanmar, the IBA sought to promote ILAM and the reform of the Bar Council Act, with ILAM being the vehicle for a national bar association and the reform of the Bar Council Act being the means to ensure that ILAM gained the power to govern lawyers independent from state control (IBA 2015b; IBA 2013a). The analysis in preceding sections, however, indicate that the disciplinary system for Myanmar lawyers encompasses more than the Bar Council Act and also include the Legal Practitioners Act, Union Judiciary Law, and the *Ethical Principles for Lawyers and Practitioners* published by the Attorney General's office. In effect, the disciplinary system in Myanmar is not embodied in just one legal instrument but rather is comprised of an architecture of power resulting from multiple legal sources inter-connected with each other in a mutually supportive structure placing lawyers under state authority in terms of both codes of conduct and institutional procedures. To the extent that lawyer discipline is under the purview of the state, it limits the extent to which professional legal organizations can be self-governing and hence the extent to which lawyers can be independent from state power. As a result, the focus on development of ILAM and reform of the Bar Council Act, while relevant and necessary, are incomplete strategies that do not go sufficiently far enough to achieve the

IBA aspirations for an independent national bar association in Myanmar. Realization of such aspirations require an expansion in scope, either by the IBA or other sympathetic actors, to undertake a broader suite of coordinated, complementary reform strategies that simultaneously reach the Legal Practitioners Act, Union Judiciary Law, and the *Ethical Principles for Lawyers and Practitioners*. All three instruments need to be adjusted to conform with international standards of professional independence represented by such entities as the ICJ or most notably for ILAM's the IBA, with codes of conduct and institutional procedures that place lawyer discipline outside of the state.

With respect to the theoretical literature on legal transplants, the scale of constraints illustrated by the preceding discussion of Myanmar's disciplinary system presents limitations on the domestic space to accommodate the transplant of foreign ideas such an independent bar association. While the IBAHRI program did produce a measure of success in forming ILAM as a national bar association and supporting the movement to reform the Bar Council Act to allow ILAM to be independent from the Myanmar state, its progress towards IBA expectations for an independent bar association is proscribed by the structure of Myanmar's disciplinary system for lawyers. The sum result of the IBAHRI program is a self-governing professional organization, but without a larger scope of legal reforms such autonomy will not constitute complete independence for Myanmar's lawyers.

To the extent that the IBAHRI program represents an IBA attempt to transplant international conceptions of an independent bar association into Myanmar, the constraints posed by the disciplinary mechanisms for advocates and pleaders present a case of domestic barriers that delimit the introduction of a legal transplant. In which case, it qualifies the work of scholars who assert the viability of legal transplantation by demonstrating a way in which domestic environments host contextual factors capable of confining activities to transplant foreign ideas. Returning to the theoretical framework of a spectrum of perspectives regarding legal transplants between the extremes represented by Watson and Legrand, the above implications have less significance for scholars like LeGrand since they already view the notion of legal transplants as problematic. The implications, however, do hold larger significance for the literature that sees legal transplantation as a recognizable phenomenon, with relevance increasing for scholarship trending towards figures like Watson, who see legal concepts as readily transferable, and Teubner, who sees transplants as involving legal irritants that incite reconstruction of legal ideas through a dynamic between external and internal forces. For the latter body of literature, in particular, the case of Myanmar's disciplinary system for lawyers shows how domestic factors limit the scope of transplant both in terms of the likelihood of transferability and the balance of forces likely to reconstruct ideas.

Conclusion and directions for further research

The work of the preceding sections relied on textual analysis of Myanmar laws and IBA, ICJ, and UN standards on lawyer discipline. While relevant for descriptive understanding and useful for informing prescriptive actions by international efforts to reform Myanmar's legal system, the above findings would be aided by further studies that build upon the present analysis. In particular, it would be useful to enrich the discussion on Myanmar laws regarding lawyer discipline with empirical work that elucidates the manner in which such laws operate to impede the exercise of professional independence by Myanmar lawyers against the state. To a degree, there was empirical work conducted by the 2012 IBA and 2013 ICJ fact-finding missions in Myanmar, both of which found evidence of historical and continuing cases indicating politically-motivated uses of Myanmar's disciplinary system to harass lawyers critical of the government (IBA 2012a; ICJ 2013). While useful, such research was tied to NGO exploratory work to prepare subsequent development agendas, and so would benefit from more scholarly approaches involving more independent approaches and current data. Alex Batesemith and Jake Stevens provide a more recent study of resistance by lawyers against the abuses of the Myanmar state (Batesmith & Stevens 2018: 11, 14-16), but it directs itself to identifying thematic elements of legal practice rather than render larger generalizable findings for Myanmar's legal system (Batesmith & Stevens 2018: 13). Additional empirical work could expand existing understanding of how Myanmar's disciplinary system operates in practice to limit lawyer independence in two ways: 1) it would be helpful to engage in-depth case studies of lawyers that have undergone the disciplinary mechanisms identified in the preceding sections to better highlight the legal claims, procedures, and arguments used to constrain Myanmar lawyers struggling against state authority, and 2) it would be useful to pursue surveys with representative population samples of lawyers sufficient to allow generalizable understanding of the scale to which Myanmar's disciplinary system is being used to proscribe the independence of Myanmar lawyers. Such empirical studies, however, would need to be treated with due caution given the continuing uncertainties for lawyers in Myanmar's ongoing political transition.

Prospectively, it would also be beneficial if future studies could ascertain the nature of negotiations between ILAM and the Myanmar government over reform of Myanmar's legal system, particularly with respect to the treatment and status of lawyers. For the present study, the negotiations to alter Myanmar laws on lawyers were of a sufficiently sensitive nature that relevant parties in ILAM, IBA, the UAGO, and the OSCU declined to comment, directing the discussion to restrict its scope to textual analysis. If future studies are able to gain access for interviews, then it would enable an expansion in the scope of study to illuminate points of debate, attendant motivations, and concomitant intentions that would enable better understanding of potential future outcomes regarding the independence of Myanmar lawyers.

The IBAHRI's work to produce ILAM advanced IBA expectations for an independent national bar association in Myanmar in the sense that ILAM is a national association for Myanmar lawyers outside of state control. The analysis of the preceding sections, however, finds that ILAM falls short of IBA standards that call for a lawyer association that holds authority over lawyer discipline separate from the state. Specifically, the analysis finds that ILAM does not alter the structural nature of Myanmar's legal system, which maintains British colonial laws that place the disciplinary system for Myanmar lawyers under state control. The structure of Myanmar's disciplinary system works against IBA expectations for disciplinary authority to reside outside the state. It also works against ICJ and UN principles that support the existence of self-governing lawyer associations. Unless international aid efforts address the laws that define the structure of Myanmar's legal system, ILAM will be unlikely to achieve IBA aspirations for an independent national bar association in Myanmar.

Disclosure statement

No potential conflict of interest was reported by the author(s).

ORCID

Jonathan Liljeblad http://orcid.org/0000-0002-8089-5531

Bibliography

Bar Council Act Amendment of 2019. (2019) Union of the Republic of Myanmar. Available at: https://www.wintpartnership.com/images/21.2019-thelawamendingforthebarcouncilact.pdf.

Bar Council Act Amendment of 1989. (1989) Union of the Republic of Myanmar. Available at: https://www.icj.org/wp-content/uploads/2014/03/Myanmar-Bar-Council-Act-and-amendments-legislation-1926-eng.pdf.

Bar Council Act of 1929. (1929) Union of the Republic of Myanmar. Available at: https://www.icj.org/wp-content/uploads/2014/03/Myanmar-Bar-Council-Act-and-amendments-legislation-1926-eng.pdf.

Batesmith, A. & Stevens, J. (2018) In the absence of the rule of law: everyday lawyering, dignity, and resistance in Myanmar's "disciplined democracy, *Social & Legal Studies*, *28*(5), pp. 1–27.

Beckstrom, J. (1973) Transplantation of legal systems, *American Journal of Comparative Law*, *21*, pp. 557.

Cairns, J. (2013) Watson, Walton, and the history of legal transplants, *Georgia Journal of International and Comparative Law*, *41*, pp. 637–696.

Cheesman, N. & San, K. M. (2014) Not just defending; advocating for Law in Myanmar, *Wisconsin International Law Journal, 31*, pp. 718–719.

Courts Manual of 1999. (1999) Myanmar Supreme Court. Available at: https://www.burmalibrary.org/docs14/Courts_Manual-ocr-en.pdf.

Crouch, M. (2014) The layers of legal development in Myanmar, in: Melissa Crouch & Tim Lindsey (Eds) *Law, Society and Transition in Myanmar* (Oxford, Hart Publishing), pp. 33–56.

Crouch, M. (2013) Asian legal transplants and rule of law reform: national human rights commission in Myanmar and Indonesia, *Hague Journal on the Rule of Law, 5*, pp. 146–177.

Dolidze, A. (2016) Bridging comparative and international law: *Amicus Curiae* participation as a vertical legal transplant, *European Journal of International Law, 26*(4), pp. 851–880.

Freedland, M. (2004) Otto Kahn-Freund (1900-1979), in: Jack Beatson & Reinhard Zimmermann (Eds) *Jurists Uprooted: German-Speaking Émigré Lawyers in Twentieth-Century Britain* (Oxford, Oxford University Press), pp. 299–324.

Gillespie, J. (2008) Towards a discursive analysis of legal transfers into developing East Asia, *International Law and Politics, 40*, pp. 657–721.

Hamson, C. J. (1956) The Istanbul conference of 1955, *International and Comparative Law Quarterly, 5*, pp. 26.

Harding, A. (2019) The legal transplants debate: getting beyond the Impasse, in: Vito Breda (Ed) *Legal Transplants in East Asia and Oceania* (Cambridge, Cambridge University Press), pp. 13–33.

Independent Lawyers' Association of Myanmar (ILAM). (2017) Available at: https://www.ilam.org.mm/en/pages/1.

International Bar Association (IBA). (2016a) *Myanmar Lawyers Attend Workshop Promoting Legal Ethics*. International Bar Association. Available at: https://www.ibanet.org/Article/NewDetail.aspx?ArticleUid=aaf379c9-100a-4403-b06b-ca659db6646f.

International Bar Association (IBA). (2016b) *IBA President and Aung San Suu Kyi Open Inaugural Meeting of Myanmar's First National Independent Lawyers' Association*. International Bar Association. Available at: https://www.ibanet.org/Article/NewDetail.aspx?ArticleUid=67923557-0f67-403c-ad67-ff04adc4ac52.

International Bar Association (IBA). (2015a) *IBAHRI and Myanmar Lawyers Prepare for First Independent Lawyers' Association Elections*. International Bar Association. Available at: https://www.ibanet.org/Article/NewDetail.aspx?ArticleUid=96554c4d-8391-4f10-9955-d5c1ba10f019.

International Bar Association (IBA). (2015b) *Myanmar, Capacity-Building 2014-2016*. International Bar Association. Available at: https://www.ibanet.org/Article/NewDetail.aspx?ArticleUid=B0DFF549-F0F3-4A90-83D5-40B902FEDBF9.

International Bar Association (IBA). (2014a) *Laws Regulating the Legal Profession: A Comparative Review from Around the World*. International Bar Association. Available at: https://www.ibanet.org/Document/Default.aspx?DocumentUid=14490A0D-F6C4-4E12-AE48-A4D730D0CDE4.

International Bar Association (IBA). (2014b) *Myanmar: IBAHRI Host Workshop on Laws Governing Legal Profession with Daw Aung San Suu Kyi*. International Bar Association. Available at: https://www.ibanet.org/Article/NewDetail.aspx?ArticleUid=5d4e7549-e00e-46ed-8c4c-2a0c421db55a.

International Bar Association (IBA). (2014c) *Myanmar Lawyers Advance in Mission to Build a Representative National Bar Association*. International Bar Association. Available at: https://www.ibanet.org/Article/NewDetail.aspx?ArticleUid=2efce9cc-5ef9-4dde-86e4-024648d54b93.

International Bar Association (IBA). (2014d) *Myanmar's Legal Profession Moves to Establish a National Bar Association.* International Bar Association. Available at: https://www.ibanet.org/Article/NewDetail.aspx?ArticleUid=4670e898-428b-440d-b986-52b35593d40d.

International Bar Association (IBA). (2014e) *Understanding Bar Associations and Their Roles and Responsibilities.* International Bar Association. Available at: https://www.ibanet.org/Document/Default.aspx?DocumentUid=6a0a6d72-09ef-4976-8cec-df30c9674f05.

International Bar Association (IBA). (2014f) *Myanmar: Major Legal Seminar on Bar Associations' Best Practices to be Hosted by IBAHRI.* Available at: https://www.ibanet.org/Article/NewDetail.aspx?ArticleUid=ce33cd81-eb78-4209-9ca2-8a9338c17327.

International Bar Association (IBA). (2013a) *Myanmar/Burma Country Visit* 2013. International Bar Association. Available at: https://www.ibanet.org/Article/NewDetail.aspx?ArticleUid=7481efba-7855-4bd2-9af7-7cf71fe1ab43.

International Bar Association (IBA). (2013b) *Panel Discussion—The Rule of Law in Myanmar: Challenges and Prospects.* International Bar Association. Available at: https://www.ibanet.org/Article/NewDetail.aspx?ArticleUid=c68828b3-9c10-48a7-a1c7-f5d394b63cc9.

International Bar Association (IBA). (2012a) *The Rule of Law in Myanmar: Challenges and Prospects.* International Bar Association. Available at: https://www.ibanet.org/Document/Default.aspx?DocumentUid=DE0EE11D-9878-4685-A20F-9A0AAF6C3F3E.

International Bar Association (IBA). (2012b) *Myanmar/Burma Fact-finding Mission.* International Bar Association. Available at: https://www.ibanet.org/Article/NewDetail.aspx?ArticleUid=DEBA1058-8D8D-47E3-B8DB-1BA2BA82E40E.

International Bar Association (IBA). (2011) *IBA International Principles on Conduct for the Legal Profession.* International Bar Association. Available at: https://www.ibanet.org/Document/Default.aspx?DocumentUid=1730FC33-6D70-4469-9B9D-8A12C319468C.

International Bar Association (IBA). (1990) *IBA Practitioners' Guide No. 1 - IBA Standards for the Independence of the Legal Profession.* International Bar Association. Available at: https://www.ibanet.org/Document/Default.aspx?DocumentUid=F68BBBA5-FD1F-426F-9AA5-48D26B5E72E7.

International Commission of Jurists (ICJ). (2013) *Right to Counsel: Independence of Lawyers in Myanmar. International Commission of Jurists.* Available at: https://www.icj.org/wp-content/uploads/2013/12/MYANMAR-Right-to-Counsel-electronic.pdf.

International Commission of Jurists (ICJ). (2004) *ICJ Practitioners' Guide No.1 – Independence of Judges, Lawyers, and Prosecutors.* Available at: https://www.icj.org/no-1-international-principles-on-the-independence-and-accountability-of-judges-lawyers-and-prosecutors/.

Kahn-Freund, O. (1978) On uses and misuses of comparative law, in: Otto Kahn-Freund (Ed) *Selected Writings* (New York, Stevens), pp. 1–27.

Kham, N. Y. (2014) *An Introduction to the Law and Judicial System of Myanmar.* National University of Singapore 2014. Available at https://law.nus.edu.sg/cals/pdfs/wps/CALS-WPS-1402.pdf.

Legal Practioners Act of 1879. (1879) Myanmar Constitutional Tribunal. Available at: https://www.myanmarconstitutionaltribunal.org.mm/lawdatabase/sites/default/files/myanmar_code/2015/07/18-1879%20Legal%20Practitioners%20Act.pdf.

Legrand, P. (1997) The impossibility of legal transplants, *The Maastricht Journal of Comparative Law*, *4*(2), pp. 111–124.

Liljeblad, J. (2019) The independent lawyers' association of Myanmar as a legal transplant: local challenges to the idea of an independent national bar association, in: Vito Breda (Ed) *Legal Transplants in East Asia and Oceania* (Cambridge, Cambridge University Press), pp. 211–230.

Miller, J. (2003) A typology of legal transplants: using Sociology, legal history, and argentine examples to explain the transplant process, *American Journal of Comparative Law*, *51*, pp. 839–886.

Myanmar Constitution 2008. (2008) Available at: https://www.burmalibrary.org/docs5/Myanmar_Constitution-2008-en.pdf.

Nelken, D. (2002) Legal transplants and beyond: of disciplines and metaphors, in: Andrew Harding & Esin Orucu (Eds) *Comparative Law in the 21st Century* (New York, Wolters Kluwer), pp. 19–34.

Nicholson, P. & Gillespie, J. (2012) Interpreting legal transfers: the implications for law and development, in: Penelope Nicholson & John Gillespie (Eds) *Law and Development and the Global Discourses of Legal Transfers* (Cambridge, Cambridge University Press), pp. 1–27.

Nicholson, P. & Low, S. (2013) Local accounts of rule of law aid: implications for donors, *Hague Journal on the Rule of Law*, *5*(1), pp. 1–43.

Rivero, J. R. (1980) Les Phenomnenes d'imitation des modeles etrangers en droit administrative, *Pages de Doctrine*, *2*, pp. 459.

Teubner, G. (1998) Legal irritants: good faith in British law or how unifying law ends up in new divergences, *The Modern Law Review*, *61*(1), pp. 11–32.

Union Attorney General's Office (UAGO). (2010) *Ethical Principles of Lawyers and Legal Practitioners: Rights, Duties, and Responsibilities*. Union Attorney General's Office. Print version on file with the author.

Union Judiciary Law 2010. (2010) State Peace and Development Council. Available at: http://hrlibrary.umn.edu/research/myanmar/Annex%20A%20-%20The%20Union%20Judiciary%20Law.pdf.

United Nations (UN). (1990) *UN Basic Principles on the Role of Lawyers Preamble*. Available at: https://www.ohchr.org/en/professionalinterest/pages/roleoflawyers.aspx.

Walton, F. (1927) The historical school of jurisprudence and transplantations of law, *Journal of Comparative Legislation and International Law*, *9*, pp. 183.

Watley, B. A. (1950) Report on the Rome conference 1950, *Journal of Comparative Legislation and International Law*, *32*, pp. 91.vn

Watson, A. (1993) *Legal transplants: an approach to comparative law* (Athens, University of Georgia Publisher).

Wise, E. (1990) The transplant of legal patterns, *American Journal of Comparative Law*, *38* (Supplement), pp. 1–22.

Evaluating the effectiveness of the lawyer disciplinary system in Japan: a study on "repeaters"

Kay-Wah Chan

ABSTRACT
A lawyer regulatory system will usually include a mechanism to discipline lawyers who have committed misconduct. Such mechanism may have different objective(s) and function(s), which may vary from jurisdictions to jurisdictions. The Japanese system seemingly has, inter alia, deterrent and educational purposes: discouraging further misconduct and/or educating lawyers to reduce recurrence of similar misconduct. This paper focuses on the deterrent function on Japanese lawyers who have been disciplined. Through an empirical analysis of the cases of lawyers who have been disciplined more than once, this paper evaluates the effectiveness of the lawyer disciplinary system in Japan in discouraging the disciplined lawyers from committing misconduct again. It also hypothesises on some of the possible contributory factor(s) for the multiple violations.

Introduction

Lawyer regulatory systems in many jurisdictions invariably have mechanisms to discipline lawyers who have committed ethical misconduct. The over-arching objective is for maintaining certain ethical standards in the profession. Deviation will result in disciplinary sanction. Zacharias (2003) has identified nine different purposes that a lawyer disciplinary system may have under the broad theme of protecting the public, such as remedial, punitive, preventive,[1] deterrent on the lawyer concerned, deterrent on other lawyers, and rehabilitative.[2]

While Zacharias's discussion is mainly based on the American system, one or more of the nine purposes that he identified may also be applicable in another jurisdiction. In Japan, a disciplinary committee member, when interviewed by a Japanese scholar, acknowledged the deterrent effect that publication of disciplinary sanctions had on lawyers (*bengoshi*) who were not being disciplined (Ishida 2017a, p. 252). If such is the case, a disciplinary sanction should also be expected to have a deterrent effect on the *bengoshi* who was being disciplined. Further, according to information published by the Japan Federation of Bar Associations (JFBA), the penalty of disbarment was imposed in a disciplinary case on the ground, inter alia, that the *bengoshi* concerned had already been disciplined with suspension from practice twice and another penalty of suspension from practice could not be expected to have any effect on preventing his misconduct (JFBA 2010a, p. 182). Although it seemed to refer to the preventive effect of disciplinary sanction, the case should actually be referring to the deterrent effect on the *bengoshi* who was being disciplined because it was referring to the sanction of suspension from practice, which may only have a preventive effect during the suspension but not beyond.

This article evaluates the effectiveness of the Japanese lawyer disciplinary system in discouraging *bengoshi* who had been disciplined from committing misconduct again. This will be achieved through an empirical analysis of the cases of *bengoshi* who have been disciplined more than once (repeaters). The article first briefly overviews the profession of *bengoshi* in Japan and its disciplinary system. Then, it explains the methodology and sources of data for the analyses which follow. Empirically analysing the repeaters' situation, the article finds that disciplinary sanctions have a weak or no deterrent effect on at least some disciplined *bengoshi* from committing misconduct again. Possible contributory factors for the repeaters' misconduct and/or multiple violations and sanctions are then explored through analyses of their cases in three aspects: the kinds of misconduct common among serious repeaters (as defined below), the extent of repetitions for the different misconduct and the severity of the penalties imposed. Based on such analyses, the paper hypothesises on some of the possible contributory factor(s) for the repeated misconduct.

The *bengoshi* profession and its disciplinary system

In Japan, while there are different kinds of legal service providers, only the *bengoshi* are full-fledged lawyers. All the other legal service providers are permitted to handle only limited types of legal work. In 2019, there were 41,118 *bengoshi* (JFBA 2019, p. 44).[3] Many of them practised in relatively small law offices, with approximately one quarter (25.2%) practising alone, 15.3% in law offices of two *bengoshi*, and 23.3% in law offices of three to five *bengoshi* (JFBA 2019, p. 72). On the other hand, five firms have more than 400 *bengoshi* each (JFBA 2019, p. 72),[4] all of which are commercial law firms. Unlike *bengoshi* in these largest law firms, many *bengoshi* are generalists (Murayama 2020, p. 772).

Bengoshi are self-regulated. An eligible person[5] who wants to practise as a *bengoshi* must join the JFBA and a local bar association in the district court jurisdictional area where his or her office is situated.[6] The JFBA is also the "head" organisation of the local bar associations in Japan, all of which are members of the JFBA. The bar associations have power and authority over admission, disciplinary action and other regulatory matters concerning the profession.

In Japan, any person may request a local bar association to discipline any of its members. Local bar associations and the JFBA also may initiate the process. Once the process is initiated, a committee called the disciplinary enforcement committee (*kōki i'inkai*)[7] will investigate the matter to consider whether to reject the request or refer it to another committee, the disciplinary action committee (*chōkai i'inkai*),[8] for examination. The *chōkai i'inkai* will decide whether a disciplinary sanction is to be imposed and, if such is the case, the appropriate penalty. These committees are made up of *bengoshi*, judges, prosecutors and "persons of learning and experience".[9] Grounds for imposition of a sanction include a violation of the regulatory legislation[10] or the articles of association of the JFBA or the *bengoshi*'s local bar association[11] and misbehaviour impairing the *bengoshi*'s own integrity. A *bengoshi* may also be disciplined for act that harmed the order or reputation of his/her local bar association. There are four possible kinds of penalty: a reprimand, a suspension from practice for a period of no more than two years, an order to withdraw from the local bar association and disbarment. A *bengoshi* subject to a withdrawal order has to withdraw from his/her local bar association. A disbarred *bengoshi* loses the right to practise for three years.

Technically, a *bengoshi* subject to a withdrawal order may register in another local bar association and continue to practise. A disbarred *bengoshi* may, after the expiry of three years, apply to re-register. However, it is unlikely that another local bar association will accept the former (Ito 2009, p. 31) and re-registration is "not automatically granted" (Ishida 2017a, p. 247). In a case, the penalty of withdrawal order had been imposed on the ground, inter alia, that it was clear the *bengoshi* would likely commit further misconduct if he were permitted to continue legal practice (JFBA 2009a, p. 139). Given such rationale provided for the decision, the committee in this case apparently considered that a *bengoshi* subject to a withdrawal order would not have the opportunity to practise any more. If a withdrawal order would generally have the effect of a *de facto* "expulsion" from the profession, a disbarment, which is considered as a more severe penalty, should also the same effect.[12]

Methodology and sources of data

As mentioned above, this paper empirically analyses the repeaters' situation. The main sources of data are publications of the JFBA. They provide official data about disciplinary actions against *bengoshi*. This paper will first analyse the statistical data contained in the *Bengoshi White Papers* that the JFBA has been publishing annually since 2002. As will be discussed below, such analysis has limitations. Therefore, a deeper investigation is also conducted through an analysis of the data available from the monthly journal of the JFBA, *Jiyū to Seigi* (*Liberty & Justice*). The JFBA publishes announcements of all cases of disciplinary sanctions in this monthly journal. Each of these announcements contains a summary of the facts of the case, the penalty that was imposed, the effective date of the disciplinary order and other information such as the disciplined *bengoshi*'s full name, registration number,[13] practice address and affiliated local bar association. A registration number is unique to a particular *bengoshi*. It is therefore possible to find out whether a *bengoshi* has been disciplined more than once by checking the JFBA's announcements of disciplinary cases in *Liberty & Justice*.[14]

Due to the volume of the cases of disciplinary sanction that were published in *Liberty & Justice*, this paper only investigates the cases that were published in the journal from its January 2002 issue to the December 2016 issue. This is considered sufficiently valid because it covers a period of 15 years and over 1,000 cases. This paper only studies disciplinary sanctions that were imposed on *bengoshi*.[15] The announcements in *Liberty & Justice* have been checked from the January 2002 issue to the December 2019 issue for any modification or cancellation of the disciplinary orders in the cases that were published in the journal from its January 2002 issue to the December 2016 issue.[16] The investigation is also occasionally supplemented by information about the disciplined *bengoshi*, such as subsequent bankruptcy or criminal conviction, that is obtained from the mass media like newspapers.

Multiple sanctions – a sign of weak deterring effect

A disciplined *bengoshi* should, after a disciplinary sanction, be fully aware that the act he/she had engaged in was not acceptable. Therefore, it may be argued that, if *bengoshi* repeated the same or similar kind of misconduct subsequent to a disciplinary sanction, it is a clear sign of the weakness or lack of deterrent effect on these *bengoshi*. However, even for those repeaters who committed different type(s) of misconduct subsequent to earlier sanction(s), the latter should act as a warning signal to encourage them to avoid committing any misconduct in the future. While a disciplinary sanction may not seem to have an educational effect regarding a different type of misconduct, it should alert the disciplined *bengoshi* that he/she in the future needs to pay careful attention to the legal ethics standards. In order to avoid committing ethical misconduct again, a *bengoshi* who had been disciplined may easily familiarise themselves with the relevant regulatory documents (such as the *Bengoshi Act* and *the Basic Rules on the Duties of Practising Lawyer*s (Basic Rules)) and learn from the disciplinary sanctions that are published in *Liberty & Justice*. Such announcements will educate them what acts constitute misconduct that will result in disciplinary sanctions.[17] The JFBA also requires *bengoshi* to attend legal ethics courses.[18] Further, any *bengoshi* should know some kinds of misconduct, such as money embezzlement or inaction, are unacceptable conduct without a need to study or learn through reading the regulatory documents or announcements in *Liberty & Justice*. Therefore, if a disciplinary sanction has a deterring effect on a disciplined *bengoshi*, such effect will be regarding his/her committing any further ethical misconduct and not merely the same kind of misconduct for which he/she had been disciplined.

However, it would be difficult to expect a disciplinary sanction to have a deterrent effect on another misconduct for which a sanction was imposed on the same day or only shortly afterwards. Similarly, an earlier sanction would not have a deterrent effect on a *bengoshi* regarding misconduct that was committed at a time before the imposition of the earlier disciplinary sanction but resulted in a subsequent sanction. Hence, if a *bengoshi* was subject to multiple sanctions that were not imposed within a very short period of time and his/her further misconduct was committed at a time subsequent to the first disciplinary sanction, we may conclude that disciplinary sanction(s) has/have weak or no deterring effect on him/her. This is irrespective of whether the misconduct in the sanctions is of the same kind or different. The next section investigates the situation of multiple sanctions in the *bengoshi* profession.

Extent of multiple sanctions

The *Bengoshi White Papers* publish various kinds of statistical data about lawyer disciplinary actions in Japan such as the number of *bengoshi* and legal professional corporations who/which had been disciplined according to the number of sanctions that a person/corporation had been subject to. This set of data provides an overview of the situation of *bengoshi*'s repeated violations. However, the data does not always contain a breakdown or differentiation between *bengoshi* and legal professional corporations.[19] There also is no information regarding the dates when the sanctions were imposed and the time when the misconduct was committed. Despite such drawback, this statistical data reveals that, in the period from January 1989 to the end of March 2019, 1162 *bengoshi* or legal professional corporations had been disciplined and 305 (more than one quarter; 26.2%) of them had been disciplined more than once (JFBA 2019, p. 177). Among these 305 *bengoshi* or legal professional corporations, 136 (44.6%) were disciplined three times or above, with three *bengoshi* or legal professional corporations having been disciplined eight times (JFBA 2019, p. 177).

Because the above analysis has limitations, this paper also studies the announcements of disciplinary cases published in *Liberty & Justice* over a period of 15 years, namely from its January 2002 issue to December 2016 issue. Cases announced in more recent issues are not covered because there may be modifications to the sanctions or even cancellation thereof after the writing of this paper. It is acknowledged that this may also happen to the cases analysed in this paper. However, the likelihood should be much lower than the cases published in 2017 or afterwards, which are still relatively recent at the time of the writing of this paper.[20]

In the period of 15 years studied, a total of 1,103 discipline cases were announced in *Liberty & Justice*. They involved 812 *bengoshi*, among whom 186 *bengoshi* (22.9%) were subject to more than one disciplinary order within the period studied.[21] These repeaters' cases (in total 477 cases) constitute 43% of the 1,103 cases in the period studied. 68, more than one-third, of the 186 repeaters were subject to more than two disciplinary orders in the period studied (collectively called "serious repeaters" below). They included two 8-time repeaters,[22] one 7-time repeater and five 5-time repeaters. However, because the data for the tally of the 186 repeaters do not include announcements published in earlier and later issues of *Liberty & Justice* outside the period studied (2002–2016), the situation may be worse.[23]

On the other hand, a close look at the detailed information about the discipline cases found that the actual situation of repeaters may be better. In some instances, a *bengoshi* was subject to more than one disciplinary sanction in a very short period of time[24] or even on the same date.[25] As discussed above, it would be difficult to expect a deterrent effect in this situation. Imposition of disciplinary orders with the same effective date is however uncommon. Among the 186 repeaters, this has happened to only seven *bengoshi*. Only two of them had no other disciplinary sanction except the two orders with the same effective date. However, an earlier sanction would not have any deterrent effect on the *bengosh*i concerned regarding his/her misconduct that was committed before the imposition of the earlier disciplinary sanction but resulted in a subsequent sanction. The announcements in *Liberty & Justice* do not always clearly describe the time when the relevant misconduct was committed, making it difficult to refine the analysis. Nevertheless, an attempt was made to identify at least those *bengosh*i among the 186 repeaters who, based on information available from the announcements, had committed further misconduct subsequent to the effective date of their first disciplinary sanction order within the period studied.[26] This exercise found no less than 90 repeaters (among them, 47 serious repeaters) having committed misconduct subsequent to the effective date of one or more earlier disciplinary sanctions. Due to a lack of clarity or details in some announcements, the above exercise may have excluded repeaters who did commit further misconduct after the first disciplinary sanction.

In addition, a *bengoshi* who was disciplined might leave the profession. If the *bengoshi* stayed in the profession, he/she might commit further misconduct and be disciplined again. As discussed above, in general, a withdrawal order or disbarment seemingly has the practical effect of "expelling" the *bengoshi* from the profession. In other words, the disciplinary sanctions prevented, instead of deterring, further ethical misconduct. Searches conducted through the online "directory" of the JFBA confirmed that 19 serious repeaters who were disbarred or subject to a withdrawal order were not in practice anymore.[27] Such penalties had also been imposed on *bengoshi* who were disciplined only once in the period studied (non-repeaters).[28] From 1988 to 2018, a total of 93 withdrawal orders and 64 disbarment sanctions had been imposed (JFBA 2005b, p. 57; JFBA 2019, p. 175). Some repeaters who were subject to lighter penalties might have left the profession too.[29] They might have lost their *bengoshi* qualification on grounds such as bankruptcy or a criminal conviction.[30] They might have passed away.[31] Some might leave the profession out of their own accord. It may be argued that disciplinary sanctions might have indirectly contributed to this because a *bengoshi* who has been disciplined may find it difficult to continue his/her practice. If a suspension sanction has been imposed, there will be a loss of income during the suspension period. On top of this, even a sanction as light as a reprimand may cause a loss of reputation, not only among the peers but also the existing and potential clients. Therefore, a disciplined *bengoshi* may suffer a reduction, if not a loss, of clientele.[32] Staying in the profession will require the *bengoshi* to bear the financial burden of bar association membership fees. Unlike some other expenses such as office rental fee which the *bengoshi* may avoid by choosing to work from home, bar association membership fees are generally unavoidable expenses. The amount may not be low when compared with *bengoshi*'s income. The annual membership fees for the different local bar associations are said to be ranging from 422,400 yen to 1,022,400 yen (Akiyama 2017, pp. 38–39).[33] A survey that the JFBA conducted on *bengoshi* in 2018 found that the respondents' average and median annual income (after deduction of expenditure) were 9.59 million yen and 6.5 million yen respectively (JFBA 2018, p. 32). However, while a disciplinary sanction may be considered as having directly or indirectly caused a *bengoshi* to quit the profession, it may only be considered as having contributed to preventing, rather than deterring, the disciplined *bengoshi* from committing further misconduct.

Why did the repeaters commit the ethical misconduct? Why did disciplinary sanctions fail to deter some *bengoshi* from further misconduct? What are the factors that contribute to the repeated or multiple violations? Understanding the answers to these questions will assist in finding solution(s) to the problem of *bengoshi*'s multiple or repeated violations. This will facilitate the reduction of misconduct in the profession, and ultimately the protection of the public and enhancement of the public's trust in the legal system. It is however beyond the scope of this article to comprehensively and thoroughly explore these issues. It, therefore, will only attempt to preliminarily explore the matter through empirical analyses of the repeaters' cases. This article will hypothesise on some of the possible factor(s) contributing to the repeaters' misconduct and their multiple violations while it acknowledges that there may be other possible contributory factors and the identified contributory factors may be attributable to other root causes.

Serious repeaters' common misconduct

Will the repeaters' misconduct and multiple violations be attributable to their personal attributes such as incompetence, carelessness and personal financial difficulty? Some personal attributes may be reflected in the kinds of misconduct that were committed. For example, we may suspect that a disciplined *bengoshi* had financial difficulty if he/she committed the misconduct of borrowing money from client, embezzling client's money or failing to pay bar association fees. Similarly, we may have suspicion about a *bengoshi*'s competence or carefulness if he/she was disciplined for the misconduct of incompetence or negligence. This section investigates the kinds of misconduct that repeaters most commonly committed. It is understood that the underlying cause(s) of a misconduct, such as financial difficulty or sickness, might last over a period of time and cause multiple violations and multiple disciplinary sanctions. It is also acknowledged that misconduct for a subsequent sanction might have been committed before an earlier sanction. As already explained above, the data for the study in this article lacks sufficient information to refine the analysis in this respect. Hence, the main focus of this section is not on analysing why disciplinary sanctions do not deter further misconduct or are weak in this aspect. It investigates why repeaters committed the misconduct through empirical analyses on, first, the kinds of misconduct that many repeaters committed and, secondly, the kinds of misconduct for which repeaters were subject to multiple disciplinary sanctions. The latter, however, may include cases where the repeaters committed the further misconduct after a prior sanction. In that situation, the analysis in this section may also shed light on the reasons for the weak deterring effect of disciplinary sanctions although this is not the main focus in this section.

First, the 241 cases that involved the 68 serious repeaters were analysed to explore whether there are some common kinds of misconduct among them. Two-time repeaters are excluded because, in the period studied, they have been disciplined twice only. It will then be followed by an exploration on the question whether there is a difference between the 21 *bengoshi* who were subject to four or more disciplinary sanctions (called "most serious repeaters" hereinafter) and the 47 three-time repeaters in the misconduct that they respectively committed. Following the methodology adopted in an earlier study on the lawyer disciplinary system in Japan (Chan 2017, pp. 630–635), this article categorises *bengoshi*'s ethical misconduct into 26 different types.[34] These 26 kinds of misconduct are compared according to the number and proportion of *bengoshi* who committed the misconduct, and the number and proportion of *bengoshi* who had been disciplined for the misconduct twice or more.[35] The results are shown in Table 1.

As shown in Table 1, four types of misconduct are clearly the most common among the serious repeaters. They are inaction or delay, money embezzlement

Table 1. Common misconduct of the serious repeaters (2002–2016).

	Serious repeaters		Most serious repeaters		3-time repeaters	
Misconduct	Number & proportion (%) of *bengoshi* disciplined for the misconduct twice or more	Number & proportion (%) of *bengoshi* who committed the misconduct	Number & proportion (%) of *bengoshi* disciplined for the misconduct twice or more	Number & proportion (%) of *bengoshi* who committed the misconduct	Number & proportion (%) of *bengoshi* disciplined for the misconduct twice or more	Number & proportion (%) of *bengoshi* who committed the misconduct
Money issue / embezzlement	21 (30.9%)	39 (57.4%)	9 (42.9%)	17 (81.0%)	12 (25.5%)	22 (46.8%)
Inaction / delay	22 (32.4%)	38 (55.9%)	8 (38.1%)	11 (52.4%)	14 (29.8%)	27 (57.4%)
Fairness / good faith	16 (23.5%)	42 (61.8%)	6 (28.6%)	14 (66.7%)	10 (21.3%)	28 (59.6%)
Failure to report (progress/outcome)	16 (23.5%)	37 (54.4%)	5 (23.8%)	15 (71.4%)	11 (23.4%)	22 (46.8%)
Acting against client's instructions / without consent	3 (4.4%)	23 (33.8%)	2 (9.5%)	8 (38.1%)	1 (2.1%)	15 (31.9%)
Improper handling	2 (2.9%)	19 (27.9%)	1 (4.8%)	9 (42.9%)	1 (2.1%)	10 (21.3%)
Collaboration with non-*bengoshi*	4 (5.9%)	13 (19.1%)	2 (9.5%)	7 (33.3%)	2 (4.3%)	6 (12.8%)
Explain/mandate on entrustment	2 (2.9%)	17 (25.0%)	0	6 (28.6%)	2 (4.3%)	11 (23.4%)
Practice during suspension	2 (2.9%)	16 (23.5%)	0	8 (38.1%)	2 (4.3%)	8 (17.0%)
Conflict of interest	2 (2.9%)	15 (22.1%)	0	6 (28.6%)	2 (4.3%)	9 (19.1%)
Legal fees	2 (2.9%)	14 (20.6%)	1 (4.8%)	4 (19.0%)	1 (2.1%)	10 (21.3%)
Not returning client's property	1 (1.5%)	13 (19.1%)	1 (4.8%)	6 (28.6%)	0	7 (14.9%)
Loan relation with client	1 (1.5%)	12 (17.6%)	1 (4.8%)	5 (23.8%)	0	7 (14.9%)
Incompetence/ negligence	2 (2.9%)	12 (17.6%)	1 (4.8%)	6 (28.6%)	1 (2.1%)	6 (12.8%)
Promoting unlawful act	0	9 (13.2%)	0	5 (23.8%)	0	4 (8.5%)
Staff supervision	1 (1.5%)	7 (10.3%)	0	4 (19.0%)	1 (2.1%)	3 (6.4%)

(*Continued*)

Table 1. Continued.

	Serious repeaters		Most serious repeaters		3-time repeaters	
Misconduct	Number & proportion (%) of *bengoshi* disciplined for the misconduct twice or more	Number & proportion (%) of *bengoshi* who committed the misconduct	Number & proportion (%) of *bengoshi* disciplined for the misconduct twice or more	Number & proportion (%) of *bengoshi* who committed the misconduct	Number & proportion (%) of *bengoshi* disciplined for the misconduct twice or more	Number & proportion (%) of *bengoshi* who committed the misconduct
Bar association fees	0	9 (13.2%)	0	3 (14.3%)	0	6 (12.8%)
Uncooperative attitude in conciliation	0	8 (11.8%)	0	3 (14.3%)	0	5 (10.6%)
Improper expression	3 (4.4%)	6 (8.8%)	0	0	3 (6.4%)	6 (12.8%)
Extreme/questionable tactics	0	4 (5.9%)	0	3 (14.3%)	0	1 (2.1%)
Lack of due diligence in criminal defence cases	0	4 (5.9%)	0	3 (14.3%)	0	1 (2.1%)
Confidentiality	0	5 (7.4%)	0	2 (9.5%)	0	3 (6.4%)
Breach of duty on storage of deposited fund	0	4 (5.9%)	0	1 (4.8%)	0	3 (6.4%)
Contacting opposite party	0	2 (2.9%)	0	0	0	2 (4.3%)
Accepting illegitimate matter	0	1 (1.5%)	0	1 (4.8%)	0	0
Private conduct	0	1 (1.5%)	0	0	0	1 (2.1%)

Note: Serious repeaters = *bengoshi* who had been disciplined three times or above; most serious repeaters = *bengoshi* disciplined four times or above; 3-time repeaters = *bengoshi* on whom three disciplinary orders had been imposed. The proportion (%) is calculated by dividing the number of serious repeaters, most serious repeaters or 3-time repeaters who were disciplined for the misconduct twice or more or who committed the misconduct (as the case may be) by the total number of serious repeaters (68), most serious repeaters (21) and 3-time repeaters (47).

or other money issue, failure in reporting progress or outcome, and a lack in fairness and/or good faith. This is the same for both the most serious repeaters and the 3-time repeaters respectively. The misconduct of money embezzlement or other money issue is the most common misconduct for the most serious repeaters. Over 80% of them committed this misconduct (Table 1). Close to 43% of the most serious repeaters were disciplined for this misconduct twice or more (Table 1). On the other hand, the misconduct of inaction or delay seems to be the most serious misconduct among 3-time repeaters. Three kinds of misconduct had not been committed by the most serious repeaters: improper expression, private misconduct and contacting opposite party. On the other hand, only one kind of misconduct had not been committed by the 3-time repeaters: accepting illegitimate matter.[36] Further, 3-time repeaters had been disciplined for 14 types of misconduct twice or more while the most serious repeaters 11 kinds (Table 1). Therefore, as compared with the 3-time repeaters, the most serious repeaters seem more focused in fewer types of misconduct. This is particularly serious for the misconduct of money embezzlement or other money issue.

However, there are different possible scenarios for repetitions in misconduct. A particular kind of misconduct may have been repeated by many *bengoshi* but each of them only once. On the other hand, a particular kind of misconduct may have been repeated by a very small number of *bengoshi* but each of them many times. Further, many *bengoshi* may have committed a particular kind of misconduct many times. Needless to say, the third scenario is the type of misconduct that is most prone to be repeated by *bengoshi* and their perpetuators are prone to be disciplined multiple times. In order to analyse the serious repeaters' cases in these aspects, the kinds of misconduct for which no serious repeaters had been disciplined twice or more are first excluded. There are 10 of them. They are promotion of unlawful act, extreme or questionable tactics, non-payment of bar association fees, lack of due diligence in criminal defence cases, uncooperative attitude in conciliation, breach of confidentiality, breach of duty on storage of deposited fund, accepting illegitimate matter, private conduct and direct contact with the opposite party. The other 16 types of misconduct are listed in Table 2.

A comparison between Tables 1 and 2 shows that the four most common kinds of misconduct are also the misconduct for which the serious repeaters were repeatedly disciplined the most. The situation is the most serious for inaction/delay and money embezzlement or other money issue. A total of seven serious repeaters had been disciplined for the misconduct of inaction or delay three times or more, one of whom even up to six times. Three serious repeaters had been disciplined for the misconduct of money embezzlement or other money issue three times or more, one of whom up to four times. In other words, their perpetrators seemingly are prone to be subject to multiple disciplinary sanctions.

Table 2. Misconduct (by number of serious repeaters and times for which they were disciplined) (2002–2016).

Misconduct	Once	Twice	3 times	4 times	5 times	6 times
Inaction / delay	16	15	6	–	–	1
Money issue / embezzlement	18	18	2	1	–	–
Fairness / good faith	26	12	4	–	–	–
Report (progress/outcome)	21	15	1	–	–	–
Collaboration with non-*bengoshi*	9	3	1	–	–	–
Legal fees	12	1	1	–	–	–
Conflict of interest	13	1	1	–	–	–
Improper expression	3	3	–	–	–	–
Incompetence / negligence	10	2	–	–	–	–
Act against client's instructions / without consent	20	3	–	–	–	–
Practise during suspension	14	2	–	–	–	–
Explain / mandate on entrustment	15	2	–	–	–	–
Improper handling	17	2	–	–	–	–
Supervision of staff	6	1	–	–	–	–
Loan relation with client	11	1	–	–	–	–
Fail to return client's property	12	1	–	–	–	–

Personal attributes

As discussed above, the kinds of misconduct committed may reflect the disciplined *bengoshi*'s personal attributes. Would the *bengoshi* who committed the misconduct of money embezzlement or other money issue be having cashflow or other financial difficulty or issues (collectively called "financial difficulty" below)? This seemingly will particularly be the case if the *bengoshi* also committed other money-related misconduct such as borrowing money from client and/or failing to pay bar association fees. In some of those incidences, financial difficulty may be one of the contributory factors for the multiple violations and/or the weak deterring effect of disciplinary sanctions.

In several examples, the *bengoshi* seem to have faced financial pressures. One *bengoshi* had been disciplined four times in the period studied. The summary of the third disciplinary sanction against him in *Liberty & Justice* revealed that he had borrowed 17 million yen from a client. For this misconduct and his violation of the provision in the Basic Rules regarding legal fees, he was reprimanded. The fourth disciplinary action against him involved three different incidences. He had borrowed from a client 2 million yen but failed to make repayment on the due date, and subsequently failed to make repayment in accordance with the agreement made during the proceedings of a conciliation that the client initiated. He had misappropriated about two million yen of another client's money that he received. Further, he failed to pay the membership fees for both the JFBA and his local bar association in the total sum of 1,363,100 yen. He was ordered to withdraw from his local bar association.

The second example also concerns a 4-time repeater. The summary of his third disciplinary case revealed that he borrowed 10 million yen from his client in February 2013 but, by the end of May 2015, still failed to make repayment. Soon after the effective date of the disciplinary sanction, he did repay his client together with late payment charge/interest. However, he was subsequently disciplined twice again for failing to return money in his custody to clients/former clients.[37] The fifth case, which was outside the period studied, also involved other misconduct. He failed to make payment within the deadline as agreed under a conciliation settlement agreement. For a period after the first discipline case, he used a different given name on his home page without notifying and obtaining approval from the JFBA. He was disbarred.

The third example concerns a 3-time repeater. In the first case, he failed to make relevant payment to his client for over 11 years. The second case involved two incidences. He had borrowed five million yen from his client but failed to make repayment by the due date as agreed in a dispute conciliation. Further, he agreed in a conciliation with another client to return money but failed to do so by the due date. In the third case, he failed to pay local bar association membership fee.

The *bengoshi* in the fourth example was also a 3-time repeater. The summary of the first case revealed that he had borrowed money for paying the expenses of joining bar association. He failed in its repayment despite promises to do so. He had also used up his client's money. Further, he persistently failed to comply with a contract to make the relevant payment. In the second case, he was disciplined for failure in payment of bar association fees. The third case concerned multiple incidences which were all related to the penalty of suspension from practice for 18 months that he received in the first case. He continued to practise notwithstanding the sanction. He did not cancel entrustment agreements[38] with existing clients and failed to return to them money in his custody. It is acknowledged that he might have continued his practice, despite the suspension, to avoid letting his clients know about his disciplinary sanction. However, given that he failed to pay bar association fee as discussed above, it is also possible that he was in need of money.

The fifth example also concerns a 3-time repeater. The misconduct in the first case was delay or inaction. In the second case, in addition to the misconduct of inaction, he had also used client's money to cover the expenditure of his law office.[39] In the third case, his misconduct included delay or inaction as well as borrowing money, a total of 950,000 yen, from a client and failure to repay this loan. His misconduct of inaction or delay might have been caused by his health issue,[40] which might also have affected his practice and financial situation such as cashflow issue. This seems to be corroborated by the fact that he had used his client's money to cover office expenditure and had borrowed money from client.

Health issues might also have affected another *bengoshi*, a 2-time repeater, in his practice and might be one of the factors that contributed to his inaction or delay in handling cases, for which he had been disciplined twice. The summary of the second case revealed that this 2-time repeater had been hospitalised. As discussed above, the misconduct of inaction or delay is another common misconduct among the serious repeaters. It is acknowledged that, in some occasions, other than health issues, there might be other factors contributing to such kind of ethical violation. Examples include acceptance of an excessive number of cases beyond what the *bengoshi* can handle and/or poor practice management.

Severity of penalty

Besides *bengoshi*'s personal attributes, the severity of penalty may also contribute to *bengoshi*'s multiple violations. Zacharias (2003, p. 691) argued that, while lawyers might "engage in some cost–benefit analysis" to compare "probable punishment" and "the benefits of" committing the misconduct, they might just be concerned with the possibility of being disciplined but would not be concerned about the likely severity of penalty. He argued that lawyers were concerned with the "damage to reputation and peer admiration" as a result of a disciplinary sanction (Zacharias 2003, p. 691). This argument may be valid for *bengoshi* who have never been disciplined. However, it seems weak regarding *bengoshi* who have been disciplined before. Their "reputation and peer admiration" would already have been damaged. A *bengoshi* who was a disciplinary committee member has stated that every *bengoshi* considered it a shame to have his or her name published in the announcement of discipline sanctions in *Liberty & Justice* (Ishida 2017a, p. 252). As illustrated in a case, a disciplinary sanction of reprimand could cause an existing client to change legal representation to another *bengoshi*.[41] If a *bengoshi* engages in a cost–benefit calculation, the severity of penalty will be relevant.

Analysis of the penalties that had been imposed on the 21 most serious repeaters reveals three phenomena that may contribute to *bengoshi*'s multiple violations and/or may have weakened the deterrent effect of disciplinary sanctions. The first phenomenon is that multiple violations do not necessarily result in any of the two heaviest penalties, namely disbarment or order to withdrawal from the local bar association. Only seven of these 21 *bengoshi* had been disbarred or subject to withdrawal orders. They were two 5-time repeaters and five 4-time repeaters. The second phenomenon is that light penalties may be imposed notwithstanding multiple sanctions. Reprimand, which is the lightest penalty, may be imposed at a fourth or sixth sanction. Four-time repeater might not have been given a penalty heavier than a suspension from practice for two months. Five-time repeaters might not have been subject to a penalty that is heavier than a suspension from practice for three or four months. Light penalties such as reprimand or a short suspension from practice may not effectively deter a disciplined *bengoshi* from further misconduct. This may also be the case for longer suspension too. A proportion of serious repeaters violated suspension sanctions (Table 1). These cases include suspension from practice for a relatively short period (such as three months) as well as much longer period (such as 18 months or two years). The suspension sanctions apparently did not deter some *bengoshi* from committing further misconduct, at least the misconduct of violating a suspension sanction. The third phenomenon is that the penalties do not necessarily become increasingly severe for repeated violations. For eight of the 21 most serious repeaters, the last sanction they received in the period studied was lighter than one or more of their prior sanctions. Three of them, two 5-time repeaters and one 4-time repeaters, are found subject to disciplinary sanction again beyond the period studied in this article when the 2017–2019 issues of *Liberty & Justice* were checked for modification or cancellation of disciplinary orders.

It is unclear whether the disciplinary committees in all cases considered the *bengoshi*'s prior disciplinary sanction(s). In some discipline cases, it was expressly mentioned that, in deciding the appropriate penalty, the committees had considered the fact that the *bengoshi* had prior disciplinary case(s).[42] However, not all announcements of disciplinary cases published in *Liberty & Justice* had such a clear mention.[43] For those cases with no mention of prior sanction(s), it is unclear whether prior sanction(s) was a factor in the determination of the appropriate penalty. On the other hand, when prior sanction(s) was/were considered, it is unclear how much weight it/they had in comparison with any other factors that the committees considered. It may be argued that, in determining the penalty, the severity and type of the misconduct are more significant factors than prior sanction(s). However, if a *bengoshi* may be merely reprimanded at the fourth or sixth sanction, the disciplinary sanction may lack strength in deterring the repeaters from further violations. When the issues of *Liberty & Justice* published between 2017 and 2019 were checked for any modification or cancellation of disciplinary orders, it was noticed that the 7-time repeater, several other serious repeaters and more than 15 two-time repeaters were disciplined again beyond the period studied in this article.[44]

Conclusion

The lawyer disciplinary system in Japan, like its counterparts in many other jurisdictions, aims to deter the disciplined lawyers from committing further misconduct. The empirical analysis above finds that it is ineffective in this respect on at least some of the *bengoshi* who had been disciplined. They committed further misconduct and were disciplined again. Some were subject to a high number of disciplinary sanctions. The most common types of misconduct that serious repeaters committed include inaction or delay and money embezzlement or other money issue. These two types of misconduct are prone to be repeated by serious repeaters. Their perpetrators seemingly are also prone to be subject to multiple disciplinary sanctions. The prevalence of the misconduct of money embezzlement or other money issue among the most serious repeaters seems to suggest that financial difficulty may be one of the factors contributing to repeaters' multiple violations and probably also the weak or lack of deterrent effect of the disciplinary sanctions on *bengoshi* who were disciplined. Financial difficulty may be attributable to sickness and/or other underlying factors. Health issues may also be a contributory factor of repeaters' misconduct and/or multiple violations.

In addition to *bengoshi*'s personal attributes, the analysis above in this article also discovers three phenomena regarding the severity of the penalties imposed on the most serious repeaters that may have contributed to *bengoshi*'s multiple violations and/or weakened the deterrent effect of disciplinary sanctions. Multiple violations do not necessarily result in any of the two heaviest penalties. Light penalties may be imposed notwithstanding multiple sanctions. The penalties do not necessarily become increasingly severe for repeated violations.

The findings in this article, as will be discussed below, are consistent with some of the arguments under the deterrence theory[45] on criminal punishment. Under this theory, the fear of punishment deters crime (Lee 2017, p. 3; Paternoster 2010, p. 766; Taxman and Piquero 1998, p. 131). Punishment fails to deter people who "do not fear punishment" (Lee 2017, pp. 12–13), for example, those who "consider punishment a price worth paying" or "feel that ... the risk worth taking" (Lee 2017, p. 14). A *bengoshi* in dire financial situation may, despite having been disciplined before, consider the risk of being disciplined again worth taking. Given the issues regarding the severity of disciplinary sanctions that are discussed above, repeaters may consider further disciplinary sanction "a price worth paying". Under the traditional deterrence theory on criminal punishment, it is crucial for punishment to be "certain" in order to deter crime (Butters *et al.* 2020, p. 23; Lee 2017, pp. 15–16; Paternoster 2010, p. 769). Criminal punishment fails to deter those people who are "confident that ... punishment will not follow ... offense" (Lee 2017, p. 15). Similarly, disciplinary sanction(s) may fail to deter a *bengoshi* from committing further misconduct if he/she thinks that he/she will not be caught again. The repeater may have such confidence if, despite having been "caught" before, many of his/her other prior misconduct had not been detected or if he/she thinks that he/she has learnt from the prior disciplinary case(s) how to avoid misconduct being detected.

Identification of the contributory factors of multiple violations will inform regulators, such as the JFBA, to explore appropriate measures. Regarding the issues of severity of disciplinary penalties on repeaters, given that bar associations have record of past sanctions and prior sanctions were mentioned in some cases, it would be appropriate for all disciplinary action committees to have such information when they decide on the appropriate penalties. If such was not the case, this should be ensured, for the purpose of equity and also consistency in the severity of penalties. Similarly, at least for the purpose of equity and consistency, the *bengoshi*'s prior disciplinary sanction(s) should always be considered when the appropriate penalty is to be decided. Some committees clearly had done this. If not already done, it should be ensured that, for misconduct of the same type and severity, repeaters will receive heavier penalties than *bengoshi* who have not been disciplined before and the penalties will become increasingly severe for repeated violations. Regarding *bengoshi*'s health issues, the JFBA and/or the local bar associations may provide relevant support, particularly for *bengoshi* who are in solo or very small practice. As discussed at the beginning of this article, many *bengoshi* are in such small practices. Compared with firms of substantial size, these very small firms may also lack effective internal mechanisms to monitor matters such as the handling of cases and custody of clients' money. It is however beyond the scope of this article to comprehensively and thoroughly analyse these issues and all the contributory factors of *bengoshi*'s multiple violations. This is left for future research.

Notes

1. He referred to "disabling" the lawyer concerned from further misconduct.
2. The other three purposes are: "enhancing the image of the profession and the way the profession practices law", "protecting the integrity of the disciplinary process" and "balancing client protection and mercy to lawyers" (see Zacharias 2003, p. 698).
3. The data is as of 31 March 2019.
4. The data is as of 31 March 2019.
5. Generally, to be eligible, the person needs to pass the National Legal Examination, receive training in the Legal Training and Research Institute and successfully graduate from this Institute.
6. Hokkaido has four district court jurisdictional regions. Each of the other 46 prefectures has one district court jurisdictional region. Each of such regions has one local bar association except Tokyo which has three.
7. Each local bar association and the JFBA have their respective *kōki i'inkai*.
8. Each local bar association and the JFBA have their respective *chōkai i'inkai*.
9. "Persons of learning and experience" are also sometimes translated as "academic experts".
10. It is the Bengoshi Act (Act No. 205, 1949).
11. The Articles of Association of the JFBA requires all *bengoshi* to comply with the rules and regulations of the JFBA, which include the major legal ethics "code": the Basic Rules on the Duties of Practising Lawyers.
12. In this respect, it should be noted Paragraph 1 of Article 12 of the Bengoshi Act stipulates that, even after the expiry of the three years, a bar association may refuse re-registration if there is a risk that the person is not fit to practice law.
13. Upon registration at the JFBA and local bar association, each *bengoshi* will be provided a registration number.
14. It is acknowledged that generally, as pointed out by Ishida (2017b, p. 57), before a revision of the Articles of Association of the JFBA in mid-2010s, when a *bengoshi* cancelled his/her registration (such as for overseas study) and re-registered afterwards, he/she would have a registration number that is different from before.

15. The tally excludes disciplinary cases against special members of the Okinawa Bar Association, foreign lawyers or legal professional corporations. From April 2002, *bengoshi* are permitted to incorporate. Disciplinary sanctions may also be imposed on legal professional corporations. Special members of the Okinawa Bar Association and foreign lawyers are not *bengoshi*.
16. Disciplinary process mostly commences at the local bar level (rather than at the JFBA level) (Ishida 2017a, pp. 246–247). Therefore, most of the disciplinary sanctions were first imposed by local bar associations. When a local bar association imposed a disciplinary sanction, the complainant may object and the disciplined *bengoshi* may appeal the case to the JFBA, which may modify the disciplinary sanction that the local bar association imposed and replace it with a different penalty. This study treats such a case as published in the calendar year in which the initial sanction order was published in *Liberty & Justice* but adopts the penalty subsequent to the modification. The JFBA may cancel the disciplinary order, in which case the *bengoshi* concerned is not disciplined. Such a case is excluded from the tally in this study. If, upon the complainant's objection, the JFBA cancelled a local bar association's no-discipline ruling and decided to discipline a *bengoshi*, this study treats this case as published in the calendar year in which the JFBA's decision was published in *Liberty & Justice*.
17. A *bengoshi* who was a disciplinary committee member has pointed out such educational effect (see Ishida 2017a, p. 252).
18. *Bengoshi* are required to attend such courses in the first year of admission and then periodically afterwards (JFBA 2019, p. 182).
19. For example, a breakdown between *bengoshi* and legal professional corporations is found in the *Bengoshi White Paper 2014* but not its subsequent editions in 2015–2019 (see JFBA 2014b, p. 195; JFBA 2015b, p. 183; JFBA 2016b, p. 163; JFBA 2017c, p. 159; JFBA 2018, p. 175; JFBA 2019, p. 177).
20. A check on the January to December 2017 issues of *Liberty & Justice* found changes in penalty or cancellation of disciplinary orders in two cases published in the 2015 issues of the journal, four cases published in its 2016 issues and three cases published in the January to November 2017 issues. A check on the January to December 2018 issues of *Liberty & Justice* found such changes or cancellation in two cases published in the 2016 issues of the journal, four cases published in its 2017 issues and three cases published in its 2018 issues. A check on the January to December 2019 issues of *Liberty & Justice* found such changes or cancellation in one case published in the 2016 issues of the journal, one case published in its 2017 issues, two cases published in its 2018 issues and two cases published in its 2019 issues. Therefore, there is a higher likelihood of further changes to cases published in the issues in 2017 or subsequent years than cases published earlier.
21. Repeaters are identified by checking the *bengoshi* registration numbers reported in the announcements. When the same registration number is found in more than one case, the *bengoshi* with such registration number is considered as a repeater. It is acknowledged that a *bengoshi* may have different registration numbers due to cancellation of registration (such as for overseas study) and subsequent re-registration. Such incidences are however uncommon. Further, without other evidence to verify the identity, *bengoshi* with different registration numbers but the same name cannot be simply treated as the same person.
22. In this article, the term "eight-time repeater" refers to a *bengoshi* who had been disciplined eight times in the period studied. It does not mean a *bengoshi* who had been disciplined nine times. Terms such as two-time repeater, three-time repeater and the like have corresponding meanings in the same manner.

23. A *bengoshi* who was disciplined only once in the period studied (non-repeater) might have been subject to one or more disciplinary orders outside the period studied. Some of the repeaters might also have been sanctioned before or after the period studied. For example, the announcement of a discipline case in *Liberty & Justice* revealed that a disciplinary sanction had been imposed on the *bengoshi* concerned, who is a repeater in the period studied in this article, before the period studied (JFBA 2006b, p. 171). Similarly, a past sanction outside the period studied was revealed in the media coverage of a case concerning another repeater (Yomiuri Shimbun 2012a, p. 37). When the 2017–2019 issues of *Liberty & Justice* were checked for modifications or cancellations of disciplinary orders, it was also noticed that some repeaters in the period studied were subsequently disciplined again (see, for example, JFBA 2015a, p. 98; JFBA 2017a, pp. 96–97) and some *bengoshi* who were disciplined only once in the period studied were also disciplined again subsequently (see for example, JFBA 2012a, p. 118; JFBA 2017a, pp. 91–92).
24. For example, a *bengoshi* was subject to a disciplinary order that was effective from 3 August 2009 and then another order that was effective from 7 September 2009 (see JFBA 2009c, p. 179; JFBA 2010a, p. 178).
25. For example, see JFBA (2009b, pp. 112–113) and JFBA (2010b, pp. 174–175).
26. A *bengoshi* might have appealed to the JFBA against a local bar association's disciplinary sanction against him or her. Similarly, a *bengoshi* may "appeal" to the Tokyo High Court regarding a disciplinary sanction imposed by the JFBA. In such situations, the effect of the disciplinary sanction may be suspended pending the result of the appeal. In this article, for each case, the effective date of sanction as stated in the announcement of the disciplinary order that was first handed down is treated as the effective date of the disciplinary sanction notwithstanding any appeal. It is because the *bengoshi* concerned should then be aware of a disciplinary sanction imposed against him or her although he or she appealed. This study excludes any case where, upon appeal, a *bengoshi* was ultimately not disciplined as far as the no-discipline decision was published in *Liberty & Justice* no later than its December 2019 issue.
27. A search was conducted on 8 February 2018 with the use of the *bengoshi*'s registration numbers. On 4 April 2018, a search was conducted again on the 19 *bengoshi* with the use of their names (not registration numbers). Both searches confirmed that the 19 *bengoshi* were not on the JFBA directory at the respective time of the searches. It is acknowledged that a *bengoshi* might change his/her name. But, the cases of a *bengoshi* having different registration numbers (due to cancellation of registration and re-registration) and different names (due to change of name) should be rare.
28. For examples of non-repeaters who were disciplined with withdrawal orders, see JFBA (2010b, pp. 175–176) and JFBA (2016a, p. 97). For an example of a non-repeater who was disbarred, see JFBA (2015a, p. 98).
29. The abovementioned searches through the online "directory" of the JFBA also found that 24 *bengoshi*, who had been disciplined three times or more but without any withdrawal or disbarment order, had left the profession.
30. Under Article 7 of the *Bengoshi Act*, a person will lose qualification as a *bengoshi* in a number of situations, such as if he/she has been sentenced to imprisonment or more severe punishment, or his/her bankruptcy proceedings have commenced and his/her civil rights have not been restored yet. For example, the JFBA cancelled the registration of a repeater after the commencement of his bankruptcy proceedings (Yomiuri Shimbun 2010, p. 17). Another repeater should have lost his *bengoshi* qualification as a result of a criminal conviction (Yomiuri Shimbun 2012b, p. 30).

31. For example, a repeater passed away in less than one year after the imposition of a disciplinary sanction, which was a suspension from practice for three months (JFBA 2017b, p. 110).
32. A *bengoshi*'s client, after learning that the *bengoshi* was disciplined, changed legal representation to another *bengoshi* (JFBA 2006a, p. 123). In the prior case, the *bengoshi* concerned was subject to the lightest penalty, reprimand (JFBA 2005a, p. 132). This already caused him the loss of a client.
33. The amount of 422,400–1,022,400 yen was equivalent to approximately 3,640–8,815 euro as of 30 April 2020.
34. For detailed description of the 26 different kinds of misconduct, see Chan 2017, pp. 630–632.
35. A disciplinary case may involve more than one kind of misconduct arising out of the same incident. In some occasions, one disciplinary sanction (therefore one announcement in *Liberty & Justice*) may have been imposed regarding multiple incidences of misconduct.
36. Article 31 of the Basic Rules prohibits a *bengoshi* from taking on a case if the manner in which it will be handled or the objective of the instruction is clearly illegitimate.
37. The fifth case was revealed when issues of *Liberty & Justice* published in 2017 were checked for any modification or cancellation of disciplinary sanctions by the JFBA regarding the cases in the period studied. It was reported in the February 2017 issue of *Liberty & Justice.*
38. Under Article 30 of the Basic Rules, subject to a few exceptions, at the time of accepting a case, the *bengoshi* must enter into a written entrustment agreement with the client unless there is a reason making the entry of such agreement difficult, in which case the agreement must be made when that reason ceases.
39. He had afterwards returned the money to the client. He had also committed other misconduct in this case.
40. The summary of the first case in *Liberty & Justice* had mentioned about his sickness. An article in the newspaper *Asahi Shimbun (2008*, p. 24) about the second case reported that he mentioned about his sickness. On the third case, an article in another newspaper (Koyashiki 2010, p. 1) reported that he had, on the ground of poor health, failed to attend the disciplinary hearing to defend or explain his case.
41. See Note 32 above.
42. For example, see JFBA (2012b, p. 121) and JFBA (2014a, p. 113).
43. For example, see JFBA (2016c, p. 98).
44. It is acknowledged that these disciplinary sanctions may have been cancelled but not detected during the writing of this article if the announcement(s) was/were not published by December 2019. It is also acknowledged that the misconduct in one or more of these cases might have been committed earlier than one or more of the repeaters' earlier sanctions.
45. The deterrence theory has been "credited" to Cesare Beccaria and Jeremy Bentham (Freeman *et al.* 2006, p. 2; and see Bruinsma 2018; Butters *et al.* 2020, p. 23; Paternoster 2010, pp. 767–772).

Acknowledgements

The author would like to thank Professor Andrew Boon, Professor Judith McMorrow and other participants at the workshop on "Regulating Lawyers through Disciplinary Systems", which was held in the International Institute for the Sociology of Law (IISL), Onati, Spain, for their valuable comments and feedback on the earlier version of this paper. The author would also like to thank the IISL for their support of the said workshop. Part of the revision of the earlier version of this paper was done when the author stayed in Waseda Law School as a visiting scholar from 23 July to 23 November 2018. The author would also like to thank Waseda Law School, Professor Yoshitaka Wada and Professor Kyoko Ishida for their support regarding his visit to Waseda Law School.

Disclosure statement

No potential conflict of interest was reported by the author(s).

ORCID

Kay-Wah Chan http://orcid.org/0000-0001-9725-2391

References

Akiyama, K. (2017) There is no work! Taking off the badges: the National Legal Examination passers' agony, in: Takarajimasha, Inc. (Ed) *Lawyers, Judges, Prosecutors – Administration of Justice is Dangerous: The Current Situation of the Elites Who Lost Authority and Justice* (Tokyo, Takarajimasha, Inc.), pp. 36–39 (in Japanese).

Asahi Shimbun (Kyoto Morning Edition). (2008) Kyoto Bar Association suspended a lawyer from practice due to his failure in response and missing the limitation period, 4 June, p. 24 (in Japanese).

Bruinsma, G. J. N. (2018) Classical theory: the emergence of deterrence theory in the age of enlightenment, in: D.S. Nagin, F.T. Cullen & C.L. Jonson (Eds) *Deterrence, Choice, and Crime: Contemporary Perspectives* (New York and London, Routledge), pp. 3–28.

Butters, R., Prince, K., Walker, A., Worwood, E. B. & Sarver, C. M. (2020) Does reducing case processing time reduce recidivism? A study of the early case resolution court, *Criminal Justice Policy Review*, 31(1), pp. 22–41.

Chan, K. (2017) What have they done wrong? An analysis of disciplinary actions against Japanese lawyers: past and present, in: K. Ageishi, H. Otsuka, K. Musashi & M. Hirayama (Eds) *The Legal Process in Contemporary Japan: A Festschrift in Honor of Professor Setsuo Miyazawa's 70th Birthday* Vol.1 (Tokyo, Shinzansha Publisher Co., Ltd), pp. 625–642.

Freeman, J., Liossis, P. & David, N. (2006) Deterrence, defiance and deviance: an investigation into a group of recidivist drink drivers' self-reported offending behaviours, *The Australian and New Zealand Journal of Criminology*, 39(1), pp. 1–19.

Ishida, K. (2017a) Deterioration or refinement? Impacts of an increasing number of lawyers on the lawyer discipline system in Japan, *International Journal of the Legal Profession*, 24 (3), pp. 243–257.

Ishida, K. (2017b) Do the young lawyers degrade the quality of legal services? An analysis from the statistical data of lawyer discipline, *Japanese Law & Society Review*, 3, pp. 49–70 (in Japanese).

Ito, A. (2009) *Study of the Bengoshi Profession* (Tokyo, Sangakusha Publishing Co., Ltd) (in Japanese).

Japan Federation of Bar Associations. (2005a) Announcements of disciplinary sanctions, *Liberty & Justice*, 56(7), pp. 128–134 (in Japanese).

Japan Federation of Bar Associations. (2005b) *Bengoshi White Paper 2005 Edition* (Tokyo, Japan Federation of Bar Associations) (in Japanese).

Japan Federation of Bar Associations. (2006a) Announcements of disciplinary sanctions, *Liberty & Justice*, 57(5), pp. 120–125 (in Japanese).

Japan Federation of Bar Associations. (2006b) Announcements of disciplinary sanctions, *Liberty & Justice*, 57(6), pp. 167–173 (in Japanese).

Japan Federation of Bar Associations. (2009a) Announcements of disciplinary sanctions, *Liberty & Justice*, 60(2), pp. 135–141 (in Japanese).

Japan Federation of Bar Associations. (2009b) Announcements of disciplinary sanctions, *Liberty & Justice*, 60(9), pp. 112–116 (in Japanese).

Japan Federation of Bar Associations. (2009c) Announcements of disciplinary sanctions, *Liberty & Justice*, 60(12), pp. 174–183 (in Japanese).

Japan Federation of Bar Associations. (2010a) Announcements of disciplinary sanctions, *Liberty & Justice*, 61(1), pp. 175–187 (in Japanese).

Japan Federation of Bar Associations. (2010b) Announcements of disciplinary sanctions, *Liberty & Justice*, 61(4), pp. 173–177 (in Japanese).

Japan Federation of Bar Associations. (2012a) Announcements of disciplinary sanctions, *Liberty & Justice*, 63(1), pp. 114–122 (in Japanese).

Japan Federation of Bar Associations. (2012b) Announcements of disciplinary sanctions, *Liberty & Justice*, 63(9), pp. 121–124 (in Japanese).

Japan Federation of Bar Associations. (2014a) Announcements of disciplinary sanctions, *Liberty & Justice*, 65(5), pp. 111–121 (in Japanese).

Japan Federation of Bar Associations. (2014b) *Bengoshi White Paper 2014 Edition* (Tokyo, Japan Federation of Bar Associations) (in Japanese).

Japan Federation of Bar Associations. (2015a) Announcements of disciplinary sanctions, *Liberty & Justice*, 66(9), pp. 97–102 (in Japanese).

Japan Federation of Bar Associations. (2015b) *Bengoshi White Paper 2015 Edition* (Tokyo, Japan Federation of Bar Associations) (in Japanese).

Japan Federation of Bar Associations. (2016a) Announcements of disciplinary sanctions, *Liberty & Justice*, 67(11), pp. 95–100 (in Japanese).

Japan Federation of Bar Associations. (2016b) *Bengoshi White Paper 2016 Edition* (Tokyo, Japan Federation of Bar Associations) (in Japanese).

Japan Federation of Bar Associations. (2016c) Announcements of disciplinary sanctions, *Liberty & Justice*, 67(12), pp. 94–100 (in Japanese).

Japan Federation of Bar Associations. (2017a) Announcements of disciplinary sanctions, *Liberty & Justice*, 68(2), pp. 90–102 (in Japanese).

Japan Federation of Bar Associations. (2017b) Registration cancellation, *Liberty & Justice*, 68 (3), pp. 110–111 (in Japanese).

Japan Federation of Bar Associations. (2017c) *Bengoshi White Paper 2017 Edition* (Tokyo, Japan Federation of Bar Associations) (in Japanese).

Japan Federation of Bar Associations. (2018) *Bengoshi White Paper 2018 Edition* (Tokyo, Japan Federation of Bar Associations) (in Japanese).

Japan Federation of Bar Associations. (2019) *Bengoshi White Paper 2019 Edition* (Tokyo, Japan Federation of Bar Associations) (in Japanese).

Koyashiki, N. (2010) Kyoto Bar Association ordered a lawyer who had left a case unattended to withdraw from the bar association, *Mainichi Shimbun*, 24 April, p. 1 (in Japanese).

Lee, H. (2017) Taking deterrence seriously: the wide-scope deterrence theory of punishment, *Criminal Justice Ethics*, 36(1), pp. 2–24.

Murayama, M. (2020) Japan: towards stratification, diversification and specialisation, in: R. L. Abel, O. Hammerslev, H. Sommerlad & U. Schultz (Eds) *Lawyers in 21st-Century Societies Vol. 1: National Reports* (Oxford, Hart Publishing), pp. 753–774.

Paternoster, R. (2010) How much do we really know about criminal deterrence?, *The Journal of Criminal Law and Criminology*, 100(3), pp. 765–824.

Taxman, F. S. & Piquero, A. (1998) On preventing drunk driving recidivism: an examination of rehabilitation and punishment approaches, *Journal of Criminal Justice*, 26(2), pp. 129–143.

Yomiuri Shimbun. (2010) An Osaka lawyer who had debt amounting to 0.3 billion yen entered into voluntary bankruptcy; he had 20 cases not handled yet, 23 April, p. 17 (in Japanese).

Yomiuri Shimbun. (2012a) Osaka Bar Association disciplined a lawyer who did not return retainer fees and suspended him from practice for two months; it was his fifth sanction, 6 June, p. 37 (in Japanese).

Yomiuri Shimbun. (2012b) A lawyer's conviction was upheld, 21 June, p. 30 (in Japanese).

Zacharias, F. C. (2003) The purposes of lawyer discipline, *William and Mary Law Review*, 45, pp. 675–745.

Managing discourse about lawyers: pro bono and professional misconduct

Helena Whalen-Bridge

ABSTRACT

The concept of pro bono has been established in a variety of countries and has developed a distinctive discourse. Aspects of this discourse have also begun to impact other areas of the law, such as mitigation in professional misconduct. However, problems can arise if aspects of one discourse are imported into others. Using the Singapore law of professional misconduct as a case study, this article utilizes concepts from discourse analysis to understand how discourse regarding lawyers can be removed from its original context and inserted into another. The article identifies two examples of pro bono discourse in the mitigation of professional misconduct, that of distinguishing law-related public service from other charitable acts and distinguishing genuine pro bono services from self-serving commercial activity. The article investigates the coherence of this pro bono discourse in the field of professional misconduct and concludes that some pro bono discourse fits its new context while others do not. The article argues for an increased awareness of how lawyer discourse potentially impacts professional regulation.

1. Introduction

Pro bono legal services have risen in numbers and prominence in a variety of countries.[1] Pro bono has developed to the point of generating its own discourse,[2] understood here as a recognized collection of ideas and expressions. Aspects of pro bono also appear to be impacting other legal subject matter, such as mitigation for professional misconduct. However, problems can arise if aspects of one discourse are imported into another, such as different areas of the law.

Using the Singapore jurisprudence of professional discipline as a case study, this article utilizes concepts from discourse analysis to understand how a discourse such as pro bono can be removed from its original context and inserted into areas where it may not fit. The article identifies two examples of pro bono discourse: (1) distinguishing law-related public service from other charitable acts, and (2) distinguishing genuine pro bono services from self-serving commercial activity. The article investigates the coherence of these aspects of pro bono discourse in professional misconduct, and it cautions against insertion of pro bono discourse in the context of professional misconduct without due consideration of both contexts.

Discourse analysis offers a means of understanding the use and re-use of concepts from one area in another, although discourse itself is notoriously difficult to define. While disagreements regarding terminology characterize most academic research, Heffer suggests that discourse is "arguably one of the most used and least agreed on terms across the social sciences".[3] Definitions of discourse are so abundant that "many linguistic books on the subject now open with a survey of definitions".[4] Discourse analysis also has different meanings in different fields, for example, linguists define "discourse" as anything larger than the sentence.[5] All definitions however have in common a "focus on specific instances or spates of language".[6]

In fields like law, discourse frequently refers to "a stream of scholarly consideration, usually written, of the issues of concern to a particular field of enquiry".[7] Legal discourse has been defined as "'an organization' of utterances 'which progresses across time' and 'aims to achieve a particular goal.'"[8] As this article addresses the use of pro bono discourse, discussion focuses on discourse as "patterns of linguistic use which can then be referred as types of discourse", such as legal discourse or the discourse of advertising.[9] Legal discourse is a recognized type of discourse,[10] and in fact law is seen as "one of the most precise and rigorously bound discourses".[11] The law field however contains highly specialized discourse communities,[12] and legal discourse includes subcategories[13] such as statutes and contracts.[14]

Most kinds of professional discourse draw "to a very considerable extent on prior discourse", as it would be "too great a cognitive load to have to continually create new discourse".[15] In the context of critical discourse analysis, i.e. discourse analysis that focuses on power relationships,[16] Blommaert explains that "the way in which language fits into context is what creates meaning, what makes it (mis)understandable to others".[17] Blommaert discusses the concept of contextualization, which comprises "all activities by participants which make relevant, maintain, revise, cancel ... any aspect of context which, in turn, is responsible for the interpretation of an utterance in its particular locus of occurrence".[18] What we would normally call interpretation or understanding is the result of contextualization processes in which text is made to fit a particular context.[19] Recontextualization occurs when we add or change meanings.[20] Entextualization refers to the process in which original discourse is lifted out of its original context and transmitted, via quote or echo, by writing it down or inserting it into another discourse.[21]

The concept of entextualization is primarily attributed to Bauman and Briggs, who argued that a unit, a text, can be lifted from its setting and then decontextualized or recontextualized in alternative contexts.[22] The participants determine "what the recontextualized text brings with it from the earlier context(s) and what emergent form, function, and meaning it is given as it is recentered".[23] Entextualization is "mostly employed to analyse the process of transformation of verbal data into a written product such as recounts, public transcripts or 'the official version of events'".[24] But as Shuy notes, although "it is common for lawyers to be concerned with smaller chunks of language that often stand out as the focus of their criminal and civil cases";[25] discourse analysis can "demonstrate how the entire language context" may put the matter in a different light,[26] by using larger language units such as schemas, agendas, speech acts, and conversational strategies.[27]

Some research in legal studies has given the concept of entextualization a broader meaning, one which is relevant to the analysis of pro bono discourse undertaken here. In the context of ayurvedic medicine and intellectual property rights, Matthew Wolfgram explored how innovations in medical knowledge by ayurvedic practitioners confounded the logic of modern intellectual property rights discourse.[28] Wolfgram defined entextualization as "how practitioners appropriate and deploy the texts and talk of expert and lay individuals and groups", but he noted that the concept of entextualization was "not limited to the writing and deployment of text but rather the appropriation, circulation, and transformation of discourse more generally (that is, it includes but is not limited to text)".[29] It is this broader notion of entextualization that is used in this article, to understand how pro bono discourse is inserted into the field of professional misconduct, and specifically into discussions of mitigation.

The status of pro bono as a discourse appears fairly well established. Daniel Maldonado has identified seven elements of global pro bono discourse.[30] Pro bono work is legal work, as opposed to other altruistic activities lawyers can do.[31] It is provided by lawyers, individuals recognized as members of the legal discipline.[32] Lawyers are not compensated for pro bono work, and it is voluntary.[33] Pro bono work should be institutionalized, i.e. not individual, occasional and informal, but permanent, formalized, and collective.[34] Pro bono work should be provided to persons with relatively few socioeconomic resources,[35] and it should be in the public interest.[36] Maldondo's study focused on particular countries in South America. Pro bono in these countries constituted a transplant which was still weak, but elite law firms created organizations "with varying degrees of institutional cohesion and efficacy to boost pro bono discourse and practice".[37] Pro bono discourse is also a transplant in Singapore, but here it can be said to have been adopted in a more widespread manner.[38] Pro bono discourse therefore, at the general and national level, has a recognized shape, which creates material for entextualization. This entextualization has the potential to be coherent, but as Blommaeart notes in the context of globalization and literacy, when texts move from one place to another what was correct in one context may become an error in another: "texts may travel easily, but the system of use, value and function in which they were produced usually does not travel with them".[39]

2. Pro bono discourse in Singapore's jurisprudence of professional misconduct

2.1. Overview of Singapore disciplinary proceedings and the role of mitigation

This article argues that pro bono discourse has entered Singapore jurisprudence via mitigation of disciplinary offenses, and so a review of Singapore's approach to disciplinary proceedings and the role of mitigation there is required. In Singapore, disciplinary proceedings reflect the fact that they differ from criminal proceedings.[40] The standard of proof in Singapore is the criminal standard of beyond a reasonable doubt, because disciplinary charges "impact adversely on the reputation as well as livelihood of the advocate and solicitor concerned".[41] However, mitigation is far less relevant in disciplinary as opposed to criminal proceedings. In disciplinary proceedings, the court is primarily concerned with protection of the public and the standing of the profession.[42] Referring to the English Court of Appeal case *Bolton v. Law Society*,[43] Singapore courts have noted that the same mitigating factors in a criminal proceeding would have less effect in a disciplinary proceeding.[44] While mitigating factors may be considered, they should only be taken into account to the extent that they do not conflict with these wider goals.[45]

Singapore caselaw has identified four sentencing objectives when the appellate Court of Three Judges determines the appropriate penalty in a case of professional discipline:[46]

(a) Upholding public confidence in the administration of justice;
(b) Safeguarding the collective interest in upholding the standing of the legal profession;
(c) Punishment of the errant solicitor for his misconduct; and
(d) Deterrence against similar offences by like-minded solicitors by leaving "no doubt as to the standards to be observed by other practitioners".

The public interest is a central concern of disciplinary proceedings.[47] The public interest includes the integrity of the administration of justice, and the courts have highlighted the particular importance of lawyers to the administration of justice.[48] The objectives stated above include aspects of the public interest in the proceedings, but when the Court of Three Judges reviews a disciplinary matter, it can also review the procedure utilized in the various stages of disciplinary proceedings, in part to ensure that that the interests of the lawyer and client have been properly investigated and protected. Therefore, there are arguably five distinct interests in the disciplinary process, comprising the interests of the parties to the complaint, referred to here as private interests, and matters protected under the rubric of public interest:

Public Interests:

- Upholding public confidence in the administration of justice;
- Upholding the standing of the legal profession; and
- Deterrence against similar offences by like-minded solicitors.

Private Interests:

- The client (and perhaps third parties) subject to the lawyer's wrongful behaviour; and
- The lawyer, including punishment of a lawyer's misconduct as well as ensuring the lawyer's right to a fair process and a just determination.

As in other jurisdictions, an important factor in the Singapore jurisprudence on disciplinary penalties is whether the case involves lawyer dishonesty.[49] Singapore academic Tan Yock Lin has observed that "where a case involves an offender of proven dishonesty, the weight to be attached to a plea in mitigation is negligible and a striking off will be the consequence as a matter of course".[50] In *Law Society of Singapore v Tham Yu Xian Rick* (1999), a solicitor had assisted a client to avoid prohibitions on foreign ownership of real estate by having a third party purchase the property and convey it to the foreigner by means of a trust deed prepared by the lawyer. The lawyer was convicted of a statutory offense and then charged in disciplinary proceedings under Legal Profession Act s. 83(2)(a) for conduct implying a defect of character.[51] In mitigation, the lawyer noted that he had not received any financial benefit beyond the usual fees, that he had made an error of judgment, and that the error was an isolated one in an 18-year career.[52] The court however observed that a lawyer allowed to practice is publicly held out as a person the public can trust, and the purpose of the disciplinary proceeding is to determine whether he can continue to be held out in that manner.[53] The court further held that the weight of mitigating factors was "virtually negligible" in a case involving dishonesty.[54] Mitigating factors have little to no relevance in these cases.[55]

The categorization of disciplinary matters into two categories, more serious cases such as lawyer dishonesty and lesser offenses, greatly clarifies the role of the public interest in the disciplinary process. The paramount question in disciplinary proceedings is not the appropriate penalty for individual transgressions, but whether the lawyer warrants continued characterization as a person fit to continue carrying the weight of the legal profession.[56] If the lawyer has engaged in proven dishonesty, this conduct demonstrates that the lawyer cannot be trusted by the public,[57] who are dependent upon lawyer honesty. The presumptive sanction for cases involving dishonesty indicating a character defect rendering the solicitor unfit for the profession will be striking off the rolls.[58] In view of this approach, the question becomes how mitigation should be viewed in lesser offenses, and in particular, how to analyze situations in which the lawyer violated professional requirements but engaged in charitable activities or pro bono legal services. It is in this context that pro bono discourse has entered jurisprudence.

2.2. Judicial analysis of mitigation in professional misconduct: managing pro bono discourse

The article addresses two examples of entextualization of pro bono discourse in the mitigation of professional misconduct: (1) distinguishing law-related public service from other charitable acts, and (2) distinguishing genuine pro bono services from self-serving commercial activity. The first example arguably comprises an unnecessary entextualization, while the second enhances understanding of mitigation in the context of professional misconduct.

2.2.1. Distinguishing legal services from other charitable acts

The first example of pro bono discourse is distinguishing law-related public service from other charitable acts, a distinction which appears in a number of Singapore cases. In *Law Society of Singapore v Ahmad Khalis bin Abdul Ghani* (2006), the lawyer had acted for an administrator of an estate in which the sole asset was a valuable piece of real estate.[59] At a meeting with his client and other beneficiaries, the other beneficiaries expressed misgivings about a sole administrator and asked whether they could appoint a co-administrator.[60] The lawyer noted the additional time and expense involved, and the beneficiaries ultimately signed a document renouncing their right to be co-administrators.[61] The lawyer's client then became the sole administrator of the estate,[62] and the other beneficiaries came to the lawyer's office to sign a waiver of sureties to the administration bond.[63] The lawyer later assisted the client to transfer the property to his sole ownership and take out a loan on the property, which was not repaid, without the knowledge of the other beneficiaries.[64]

In disciplinary proceedings, the lawyer admitted[65] and was found guilty of falsely declaring that signatories to the consent to waive sureties had personally appeared before him.[66] The court also found that the lawyer had failed to discharge his duties as solicitor for the estate to the beneficiaries, and/or failed to safeguard the interests of the beneficiaries, in that he subordinated the interests of the beneficiaries to the interests of his client the administrator. While there had been no dishonesty,[67] in the sense of working with his client to take something from the other beneficiaries, the court found that there was an implied retainer between the lawyer and the beneficiaries,[68] and that the lawyer had failed to keep all the beneficiaries updated and had engaged in a conflict of interest.[69]

When considering mitigation during the penalty phase, the court observed that the lawyer had made "numerous (and significant) contributions" which were in the "public arena, and which were outside the law as such".[70] The court opined that these contributions were

> especially relevant in the light of the fact that they have enhanced the public well-being and do therefore correspondingly mitigate any harm that might result to the public interest as a result of the respondent's conviction under the two charges referred to above.[71]

The court also noted the "glowing testimonials tendered" for the lawyer by his peers.[72] The court appeared to take this mitigation into account, although it did not parse the particular value attributed to different mitigating factors.

Pro bono discourse arguably arises in *Ahmad Khalis'* mitigation analysis in the distinction between types of public service: public service which is outside of the law, i.e. general charitable acts, as opposed to law-related public service. There is no explanation of why this distinction would be relevant in professional misconduct, but Maldonado recognizes it as an aspect of pro bono discourse.[73] The distinction is arguably a key part of pro bono definitions, which require the provision of legal services as opposed to charitable acts generally. One influential standard are the American Bar Association (ABA) Model Rules, and Rule 6.1, "Voluntary Pro Bono Publico Service", states:[74]

> Every lawyer has a professional responsibility to provide legal services to those unable to pay. A lawyer should aspire to render at least (50) hours of pro bono publico legal services per year.

The Australian Pro Bono Centre offers extensive resources regarding pro bono.[75] Their definition of pro bono restricts pro bono services to law-related activity, such as giving "legal assistance for free or at a substantially reduced fee" to needy or worthwhile individuals or groups, conducting "law reform and policy work", providing "free community legal education", or providing a lawyer on secondment to an appropriate organization.[76]

Singapore pro bono discourse also adopts this distinction. Law Society Pro Bono Services, the organization that works with the Singapore Law Society to promote pro bono, states that the "Pro Bono Services Office is an initiative by the Law Society of Singapore to help bring free legal assistance to those in need in our community."[77] In the subsidiary legislation that governs Singapore's mandatory pro bono reporting requirement, "relevant law-related service" is defined as "providing legal advice or assistance in connection with the application of the law or legal representation in any form of legal dispute, or any other service the provision of which requires legal knowledge … ."[78] Pro bono discourse then distinguishes quite clearly between the legal or law-related services which count as pro bono, and the charitable acts that do not require legal knowledge or training which do not count as pro bono.

Law-related service is valued more highly than general community service in pro bono discourse because it supports access to justice, while volunteering for charitable projects or good causes may not. Maldonado notes that global pro bono discourse requires pro bono to serve the public interest, and while pro bono discourse does not interpret public interest in a single way, it is typically associated with activities that protect the rights of individuals or a small group of individuals.[79] The precise public interest supported by pro bono is not necessarily stated in key pro bono documents, but it is implied in for example ABA Model Rule 6.1(a), "Voluntary Pro Bono Publico Service". The rule establishes an aspirational guideline of 50 pro bono hours a year, and in carrying out this goal, the lawyer should provide the majority of hours to:[80]

(1) persons of limited means or
(2) charitable, religious, civic, community, governmental and educational organizations in matters which are designed primarily to address the needs of persons of limited means...

The Comment to Rule 6.1 states that

> [p]aragraphs (a)(1) and (2) recognize the critical need for legal services that exists among persons of limited means by providing that a substantial majority of the legal services rendered annually to the disadvantaged be furnished without fee or expectation of fee.[81]

The public interest alluded to in Rule 6.1 is essentially access to justice for persons who cannot afford a lawyer. The Australian Pro Bono Centre is somewhat clearer that pro bono serves a public interest. Their definition of pro bono states that "'Pro bono' comes from the Latin phrase 'pro bono publico' which means 'for the public good'".[82] The public interest is also reflected throughout the definition of pro bono, for example in providing legal assistance. Here pro bono is defined as:[83]

(1) Giving legal assistance for free or at a substantially reduced fee to: -
  (a) individuals who can demonstrate a need for legal assistance but cannot obtain Legal Aid or otherwise access the legal system without incurring significant financial hardship; or
  (b) individuals or organizations whose matter raises an issue of public interest which would not otherwise be pursued; or
  (c) charities or other non-profit organizations which work on behalf of low income or disadvantaged members of the community or for the public good...

Singapore sources also suggest that pro bono is strongly tied to access to justice.[84] For example, the Law Society Pro Bono Services states that it is "an initiative by the Law Society of Singapore", and that it is "part of the Law Society's stated mission to ensure access to justice for all."[85]

At a minimum, pro bono discourse restricts pro bono to law-related legal activity, because this kind of activity supports access to justice. *Ahmad Khalis*' distinction between public service within and outside of the law appears to have entextualized the distinction between law-related services and other types of community service, but it is not clear why the distinction between pro bono and community service would be noteworthy in a disciplinary context. Assuming a court would take any mitigation into account, both activities serve the public interest, one serves the access to justice aspect of the public interest, and the other serves a more general public interest. It is difficult to say that categorization as one or the other is relevant in this context.

The distinction between activities inside and outside of the law was continued in *Law Society of Singapore v Chung Ting Fai* (2006), and it might have created confusion in the evaluation of public service as mitigation, but the court went on to establish that the two types of activities have equivalent value in disciplinary proceedings. The lawyer in this case represented a husband in divorce proceedings. The husband instructed the lawyer that he would agree to give the wife custody and care of their child, but he wanted to contest all other issues such as division of matrimonial assets and maintenance of the wife and child.[86] At the relevant hearing, one of the firm's legal assistants carried out the husband's instructions,[87] but the law firm secretary drafting the order misunderstood the legal assistant's notes from the hearing[88] and drafted the order incorrectly, stating that the parties had consented to disposition of the matrimonial household and maintenance. The lawyer did not notice the error and the order was submitted to the court and issued.[89] The lawyer asserted that he raised the possibility of appeal by requesting an extension of time and agreeing to waive the charges.[90] The husband then came into the lawyer's office to sign an affidavit to support the request,[91] but he objected to the affidavit as it contained errors and matters which had not occurred.[92] Specifically, the affidavit asked the husband to assert that he did not instruct the lawyer to file the appeal in a timely manner because he did not understand English, and that as the lawyer's office was closed for a holiday, a friend he asked to explain documents to him did so incorrectly.[93] None of these matters had actually occurred. The lawyer was charged with preparing an affidavit containing false information and advising his client to sign that affidavit for use in a court of law in contravention of the LPA, s 83(2)(h).

The court found that the lawyer's motivation in preparing the affidavit was not to avoid a malpractice action by the client, but rather that the lawyer wanted to give the client the best chance at gaining the extension of time so the appeal could be pursued.[94] The court observed that there was no evidence of dishonest intent, and that excess zeal on the client's behalf motivated the lawyer, although the actions bordered on recklessness.[95] In determining the sentence, the court noted that if the affidavit had been filed with the court, it would have constituted a deception on the court, but in fact the affidavit had not been finalized or filed.[96] Regarding the public interest, the court noted that the lawyer's peers had submitted "glowing testimonials" as evidence of positive impact in the "sphere of public service".[97] The court held that, other things being equal, public service ought to be a mitigating factor, even if it takes place outside the legal arena, "as it often does".[98] This analysis continues to reflects pro bono discourse's distinction between legal and non-legal public service, even though the relevance of the distinction is not clear. The court did state that "both types of contributions are equally important",[99] presumedly because they both serve aspects of the public interest. However, the continued distinction between legal and non-legal public service in this case arguably reflects the vitality of pro bono discourse more strongly than the prior case, because the distinction is maintained even after its relevance is diminished.

2.2.2. Genuine pro bono services as opposed to self-serving commercial activity

A second example of entextualization of pro bono discourse in SIngapore jurisprudence concerns the need to determine the value of pro bono services asserted in mitigation of professional misconduct. In *Law Society of Singapore v Tan Phuay Khiang* (2007), the lawyer represented a couple in the sale of their flat but was found guilty of conflict of interest and not protecting the clients' interests.[100] The couple had a rudimentary primary education.[101] The couple first went to a housing agent to sell the flat, and the agent informed them that they needed to purchase a new flat before they could sell the old one.[102] The agent drew up a financial plan which appeared to give the couple an excess of $90,000, and the couple agreed to proceed.[103] The couple was informed of an opportunity to purchase a new flat, but this required a cash payment of $45,000 that the couple did not have.[104] The agent advised the couple that he could arrange a loan with a licensed moneylender.[105] The couple accompanied the agent to the moneylender, who agreed to loan them the money if they signed some legal documents at the moneylender's lawyer's office.[106] The moneylender stated the interest would be a flat rate of $7,000 on top of the $45,000 principle, for a total of $52,000. The couple agreed but were handed documents stating the loaned amount to be $65,000; the agent and the moneylender explained this discrepancy by asserting that it was standard procedure for the amount loaned to be different from the amount disbursed.[107]

The couple then proceeded to the respondent lawyer's office. Upon the lawyer's instructions, they signed a power of attorney appointing a Mr. Cheung, someone unknown to the couple, as the couple's lawyer for the sale and subletting of the flat.[108] Upon completing the power of attorney, the couple were taken by the first agent to a bank branch, where a representative from the moneylender handed a check for $60,000 to the teller.[109] The money lender representative took $15,000, and gave the remaining $45,000 to the housing agent to pay for the new flat.[110] The housing agent was never able to sell the flat for the couple, so they appointed another agent, who sold the flat for $258,000.[111] A check for the amount due to the couple after legitimate deductions, $142,694.11, was forwarded to the lawyer's representative.[112] A meeting was then held between the couple, the first housing agent and the lawyer, at which the lawyer handed the wife a cheque for a mere $48.11.[113] When the wife queried the "paltry" amount, the first housing agent handed them a cheque for $86,461;[114] this cheque was dishonoured and never fully paid.[115] The couple were then asked to sign a statutory declaration authoring the lawyer to make a list payments in the thousands of dollars to various parties, some of which the couple did not know,[116] and to acknowledge that they had received a payment of $48.11, which represented the sum total of what they were owed.[117] The couple eventually requested a copy of the documents related to the loan from the lawyer, who failed to respond and delayed for 10 months.[118] When the couple received and read all the documents, they learned that the lawyer had prepared the documents, and he was supposed to represent them in the sale of the flat and disburse sales proceeds to various persons, but they did not understand why the housing agent had given them a cheque instead of the lawyer.[119] At that point, they filed a complaint with the Law Society.

The court found that the lawyer in this case repeatedly failed in his duty to advance the couple's interests.[120] The lawyer compromised their interests, and subordinated their interests to his and perhaps the other payees, in the statutory declaration.[121] The lawyer had previously acted for two of the payees, and one of the payees had referred work to the lawyer, but the lawyer did not disclose this actual or potential conflict of interest.[122] The lawyer also failed to enquire or explain the reason for the payments in the statutory declaration. Overall, the court found that the lawyer allowed his personal interest in receiving future referrals from the payees, and the immediate interest of the payees, to take precedence over the clients' interests.[123] The court noted the seriousness of these offenses, which violated the lawyer's duty of unflinching loyalty to the client.[124] This duty required the lawyer to place client interests above his own and third parties. The court also found fault with the lawyer acting for the couple in the sale of the flat, because the couple did not need a lawyer and could have relied on an administrative agency for a substantial cost savings.[125] The lawyer did not advise the couple about this. The court found that the lawyer was "indifferent" to the couple's interests,[126] and that he had been motivated solely by self-interest and preservation, the declaration being "clumsily executed for the primary purpose of immunising the respondent (and perhaps the other payees) from the consequences of his serious professional lapse".[127] The court found that "public confidence in the legal profession has been diminished" by this and other cases of errant lawyers involving substantial referrals of work from housing agents and credit companies.[128]

When considering the appropriate penalty and mitigation, the court noted that the defendant had performed the following public service:[129]

(a) assisting the Law Society by contributing articles for publication in the Chinese newspapers during the Severe Acute Respiratory Syndrome (SARS) period in 2003;
(b) serving the Singapore Armed Forces Reservist Association (SAFRA) as a volunteer lawyer providing members with free legal advice for around ten years until 2005/2006; and
(c) serving in the Citizens' Consultative Committee and as a volunteer lawyer in grassroots organizations for around five years until 2002.

In this case, the court rejected the lawyer's community service as mitigation, and its analysis again draws upon definitions of pro bono within pro bono discourse. The court noted that contributions to public service may be taken into mitigating account as a discretionary matter,[130] and it was not impressed with the defendant's public service. The court noted that public service was "a nebulous concept" and that not every act of purported public service warranted a lesser sentence.[131] The court stated that it could be concluded that "these acts had not been cloaked with altruism but rather were primarily designed to promote [the lawyer's] legal practice".[132] Since the lawyer's community service and pro bono legal services primarily served the lawyer's self-interested goals, it had little mitigation value because it did not serve the public interest in a way relevant to mitigation in disciplinary processes.

This analysis is consistent with the pro bono discourse that identifies a lawyer's motivation for doing pro bono as a prominent aspect of pro bono definitions. Comment 4 to ABA Model Rule 6.1 states that because "service must be provided without fee or expectation of fee, the intent of the lawyer to render free legal services is essential for the work performed to fall within the meaning" of the pro bono rule.[133] The Australian Pro Bono Centre's Definition of Pro Bono notes that it would not be considered pro bono to provide free first consultations with clients who are then billed at a firm's normal rates.[134] Singapore materials also recognize that in contrast to pro bono being a higher calling, the provision of free legal advice can be an improper method of soliciting paying work.[135] The Singapore Legal Profession (Professional Conduct) Rules 2015 prohibit lawyers providing free legal advice at facilities established to provide legal assistance to members of the public from distributing business cards or brochures regarding the lawyer's or the lawyer's law firm, or from acting for such a person unless the representation is pro bono.[136] Lawyer motivation when providing free law-related service has been entextualized from pro bono discourse into the mitigation of professional misconduct, but compared to the first example that distinguished between non-law and law-related public service, this example has greater coherence. To have value as mitigation in professional misconduct, the activity would have to serve some public interest, as opposed to the commercial interest of the lawyer. This goal is consistent with pro bono discourse where the primary public interest is access to justice and promoting the rights of individuals, as opposed to promoting the lawyer's business. This example demonstrates that pro bono discourse can be coherently entextualized in professional misconduct, as long as the context for both uses is evaluated and deemed relevant.

3. Conclusion

The adoption of pro bono concepts and the acceptance of a lawyer's obligation to support access to justice are important developments in professional regulation, and the existence of a pro bono discourse underscores the degree to which concepts of pro bono have gained widespread acceptance. The strength of pro bono discourse can though cause conceptual difficulties if it is entextualized without due consideration of both the original and the new context. This article has considered just two examples of entextualization regarding the mitigation of professional misconduct, but the examples indicate that pro bono discourse has the potential to complicate or enlighten analysis in the disciplinary context. The examples also suggest that there is a need for greater awareness of how lawyer discourse potentially impacts professional regulation.

Notes

1. See Cummings, S.L., De Sa E Silva, F. & Trubek, L. (2021) *Global Pro Bono: Causes, Context, and Contestation* (Cambridge); Whalen-Bridge, H. (2014) The conceptualisation of pro bono in Singapore, *Asian Journal of Comparative Law*; Cummings, S. (2004) The politics of pro bono, *UCLA Law Review*, 52; and Boon, A. & Whyte, A. (1999) "Charity and beating begins at home": the aetiology of the new culture of pro bono publico, *Legal Ethics*, 2(2).
2. Maldonado, D. (2020) The mandarins of the law: pro bono legal work from a comparative perspective, *Indiana Journal of Global Legal Studies*, 27 .
3. Heffer, C. (2005) *The Language of Jury Trial: A Corpus-Aided Analysis of Legal-Lay Discourse* (London: Palgrave Macmillan), p. 3.
4. Schiffren, D., Tannen D. & Hamilton, H. (2015) *The Handbook of Discourse Analysis*, 2nd ed. (John Wiley & Sons). (2013), Introduction to the First Edition (2005), p. 1.
5. *Ibid.*
6. *Ibid.*
7. Conley, J. & O'Barr, W. (1990) *Rules versus relationships: the ethnography of legal discourse* (Chicago: University of Chicago Press), p. 2, cited by Heffer, 2005, p. 4.
8. Little, L. (2009) Characterization and legal discourse, *Journal of the Association of Legal Writing Directors*, 6, p. 122, n. 4, citing Jean Caron (1992), *An Introduction to Psycholinguistics*, trans. Tim Pownall (Toronto), p. 153.
9. Heffer 2005, p. 4.

10. Goodrich, P. (1987) *Legal Discourse Studies in Linguistics, Rhetoric and Legal Analysis* (London: Palgrave Macmillan); Heffer, 2005, p. 4; Bhatia, V.K., Candlin, C.N. & Engberg, J. (Eds.) (2008) *Legal Discourse Across Cultures and Systems, with the Assistance of Jane Lung* (Hong Kong: Hong Kong University Press).
11. Hanny, C. (2016) Imagining new social legal futures: a sociologuistic analysis of pre-law students' experiences with discourse communities of legal practice, *International Journal of Semiotics and Law*, 29, pp. 87–120 at 88.
12. *Ibid.*
13. Shuy, R. (2015) *Discourse Analysis in the Legal Context, The Handbook of Discourse Analysis*, 2nd ed. (John Wiley & Sons), p. 823.
14. Trosborg, A. (1997) *Rhetorical Strategies in Legal Language: Discourse Analysis of Statutes and Contracts* (Tubingen: Narr).
15. Heffer, 2005, p. 10.
16. Blommaert, J. (2005) *Discourse: A Critical Introduction* (Cambridge; New York: Cambridge University Press), p. 1.
17. Blommaert, 2005, p. 39–40.
18. Blommaert, 2005, p. 41, referencing Gumperz, J., per Auer, P. (1992) Introduction: John Gumperz' approach to contextualization, in Peter Auer and Aldo DiLuzio (eds.), *The Contextualization of Language* (Amsterdam: John Benjamins), p. 4.
19. Blommaert, 2005, p. 42–43.
20. Blommaert, 2005, p. 46.
21. Blommaert, 2005, p. 47.
22. Bauman, R. & Briggs, C. (1990) Poetics and performance as critical perspectives on language and social life, *Annual Review of Anthropology*, 19, pp. 59–88, p. 73, 74; see also Silverstein, M. & Urban, G. (1996) *Natural Histories of Discourse* (Chicago: University of Chicago Press).
23. Bauman and Briggs, 1990, p. 75.
24. Frade, C. (2015) Legal translation in Brazil: an entextualisation approach, *International Journal for the Semiotics of Law*, 28, pp. 107–124, p. 109.
25. Shuy, 2015, p. 823.
26. *Ibid.*
27. Shuy, 2015, p. 824.
28. Wolfgram, M. (2012) The entextualisation of ayurveda as intellectual property, *International Journal of Cultural Property*, 19, pp. 313–343.
29. Wolfgram, 2012, p. 315.
30. Maldonado, 2020, pp. 138–142.
31. Maldonado, 2020, p. 138.
32. Maldonado, 2020, p. 139.
33. Maldonado, 2020, pp. 139–140.
34. Maldonado, 2020, pp.140–141.
35. Maldonado, 2020, p. 141.
36. Maldonado, 2020, pp. 141–142.
37. Maldonado, 2020, pp. 152–153.
38. Whalen-Bridge, H. (2014) The conceptualisation of pro bono in Singapore, *Asian Journal of Comparative Law*, pp. 97–143.
39. Blommaert, 2008, p. 6.
40. Pinsler, J. (2007) *Ethics and Professional Responsibility: A Code for the Advocate and Solicitor* (Singapore: Academy Publishing), para. 01–083, although per the Singapore courts, disciplinary proceedings are quasi-criminal in nature, *Law Society of Singapore v Chong Wai Yen Michael* [2012] SGHC 9, [2012] 2 SLR 113 at [44]

41. *Law Society of Singapore v Ahmad Khalis bin Abdul Ghani* [2006] SGHC 143, [2006] 4 SLR(R) 308, para. 6.
42. See *Law Society of Singapore v Ezekiel Peter Latimer* [2019] SGHC 92, [2019] 4 SLR 1427 at [46]; Pinsler, 2007, para. 01–084; Tan, Y.L. (2000–2001) Sentencing for legal professional misconduct, *Singapore Law Review*, pp. 69–78.
43. *Bolton v. Law Society* [1994] WLR 512.
44. *Law Society of Singapore v Tham Yu Xian Rick* [1999] SGHC 213; [1999] 3 SLR(R) 68, para. 22.
45. See Tan, Y.L. (1998) *The Law of Advocates and Solicitors in Singapore and West Malaysia*, 2nd ed. (Singapore: Butterworths Asia), para. 906–908, citing *Re Knight Glenn Jeyasingam* [1994] 3 SLR 531, 537, and *Law Society of Singapore v Wee Wei Fen* [1999] 3 SLR(R) 559 at para. 39.
46. *Law Society of Singapore v Udeh Kumar s/o Sethuraju* [2017] SGHC 141, para. 86.
47. *Law Society of Singapore v Ravindra Samuel* [1999] SGHC 28, [1999] 1 SLR(R) 266, para. 11–12.
48. *Ahmad Khalis* (2006), para. 5.
49. *Udeh Kumar* (2017), para. 101-104.
50. Tan, Y.L. (2004), *Singapore Academy of Law Annual Review*, para. 18.35.
51. *Tham* (1999), para. 9, 10.
52. *Tham* (1999), para. 19.
53. *Tham* (1999), para. 22.
54. *Ibid.*
55. See *Udeh Kumar* (2017). para. 102.
56. *Ravindra Samuel* (1999), para. 13.
57. Tan, Y.L. (2012), *Singapore Academy of Law Annual Review of Legal Profession*, 13, para. 21.3.
58. *Law Society of Singapore v. Chia Choon Yang*, [2018] SGHC 174, [2018] 3 SLR 1068 at para. 20.
59. *Ahmad Khalis* (2006), para. 11.
60. *Ahmad Khalis* (2006), para. 14.
61. *Ibid.*
62. *Ahmad Khalis* (2006), para. 15.
63. *Ahmad Khalis* (2006), para. 16.
64. *Ahmad Khalis* (2006), para. 17–21.
65. *Ahmad Khalis* (2006), para. 31.
66. *Ahmad Khalis* (2006), para. 85.
67. *Ahmad Khalis* (2006), para. 35.
68. *Ahmad Khalis* (2006), para. 73.
69. *Ahmad Khalis* (2006), para. 74.
70. *Ahmad Khalis* (2006), para. 86.
71. *Ibid.*
72. *Ibid.*
73. Maldonado, 2020, p. 138–139.
74. American Bar Association Model Rules, rule 6.1, "Voluntary Pro Bono Publico Service", https://www.americanbar.org/groups/probono_public_service/policy/aba_model_rule_6_1/#:~:text=Voluntary%20Pro%20Bono%20Publico%20Service,-Every%20lawyer%20has&text=(3)%20participation%20in%20activities%20for,to%20persons%20of%20limited%20means.
75. Australian Pro Bono Centre, https://www.probonocentre.org.au/.

76. Australian Pro Bono Centre The Australian Pro Bono Centre's Definition of Pro Bono, https://www.probonocentre.org.au/information-on-pro-bono/definition/.
77. Law Society Pro Bono Services, About Us, https://www.lawsocprobono.org/Pages/About-Us.aspx.
78. Legal Profession (Mandatory Reporting of Specified Pro Bono Services) Rules 2015, r 2, Definitions.
79. Maldonado, 2020, at 141–142.
80. American Bar Association Model Rules, "Voluntary Pro Bono Publico Service", Rule 6.1(a)(1) and 6.1(a)(2).
81. American Bar Association Model Rules, "Voluntary Pro Bono Publico Service", Rule 6.1, Comment.
82. Australian Pro Bono Centre The Australian Pro Bono Centre's Definition of Pro Bono.
83. *Ibid.*
84. See *Conceptualisation of Pro Bono in Singapore*, pp. 130–138.
85. Law Society Pro Bono Services, About Us, https://www.lawsocprobono.org/Pages/About-Us.aspx.
86. *Law Society of Singapore v Chung Ting Fai* [2006] SGHC 167, [2006] 4 SLR(R) 587, para. 8.
87. *Chung Ting Fai* (2006), para. 11.
88. *Chung Ting Fai* (2006), para. 12.
89. *Ibid.*
90. *Chung Ting Fai* (2006), para. 20.
91. *Chung Ting Fai* (2006), para. 23.
92. *Chung Ting Fai* (2006), para. 24, 25.
93. *Chung Ting Fai* (2006), para. 23.
94. *Chung Ting Fai* (2006), para. 34, 35.
95. *Chung Ting Fai* (2006), para. 35.
96. *Chung Ting Fai* (2006), para. 37.
97. *Chung Ting Fai* (2006), para. 38.
98. *Chung Ting Fai* (2006), para. 39.
99. *Chung Ting Fai* (2006), para. 43; see also to *Law Society of Singapore v Seah Li Ming Edwin* [2007] SGHC 35, [2007] 3 SLR(R) 401 at [31], which endorsed *Chung Ting Fai*'s approach.
100. *Law Society of Singapore v Tan Phuay Khiang* [2007] SGHC 83, [2007] 3 SLR(R) 477.
101. *Tan Phuay Khiang* (2007), para. 4.
102. *Tan Phuay Khiang* (2007), para. 5.
103. *Ibid.*
104. *Tan Phuay Khiang* (2007), para. 6.
105. *Ibid.*
106. *Tan Phuay Khiang* (2007), para. 7.
107. *Ibid.*
108. *Tan Phuay Khiang* (2007), para. 8.
109. *Tan Phuay Khiang* (2007), para. 9.
110. *Ibid.*
111. *Tan Phuay Khiang* (2007), para. 11.
112. *Ibid.*
113. *Tan Phuay Khiang* (2007), para. 12.
114. *Ibid.*
115. *Tan Phuay Khiang* (2007), para. 14.

116. *Tan Phuay Khiang* (2007), para. 12.
117. *Tan Phuay Khiang* (2007), para. 13.
118. *Tan Phuay Khiang* (2007), para. 15.
119. *Tan Phuay Khiang* (2007), para. 16.
120. *Tan Phuay Khiang* (2007), para. 64.
121. *Ibid.*
122. *Ibid.*
123. *Ibid.*
124. *Tan Phuay Khiang* (2007), para. 62.
125. *Tan Phuay Khiang* (2007), para. 65.
126. *Tan Phuay Khiang* (2007), para. 66.
127. *Tan Phuay Khiang* (2007), para. 70.
128. *Tan Phuay Khiang* (2007), para. 118, 117.
129. *Tan Phuay Khiang* (2007), para. 107.
130. *Tan Phuay Khiang* (2007), para. 109.
131. *Tan Phuay Khiang* (2007), para. 110.
132. *Ibid.*
133. American Bar Association Model Rules, "Voluntary Pro Bono Publico Service", Rule 6.1, Comment.
134. Australian Pro Bono Centre The Australian Pro Bono Centre's Definition of Pro Bono.
135. Chen, A. & Whalen-Bridge, H. (2016) *Understanding Lawyers' Ethics in Singapore* (Singapore: LexisNexis), para. 9.31.
136. Legal Profession (Professional Conduct) Rules 2015, r 47.

Disclosure statement

No potential conflict of interest was reported by the author(s).

Funding

This work was funded by Singapore Ministry of Education Academic Research Fund (AcRF) Tier 1, Grant no. R-241-000-185-115.

ORCID

Helena Whalen-Bridge http://orcid.org/0000-0003-1067-4001

Index

Note: Figures are indicated by *italics*. Tables are indicated by **bold**. Endnotes are indicated by the page number followed by 'n' and the endnote number e.g., 20n1 refers to endnote 1 on page 20.